On Your Confirmation

Promises for Girls

FROM THE NEW INTERNATIONAL VERSION

inspirio™

Dear Confirmand:

In the past, you may have related to God in a family kind of way. You accepted certain truths about God because your parents and other caring adults accept them. That was a pleasing thing to God, who has instructed you to "honor your father and mother" (Matthew 15:4).

Now that you've completed your Christian confirmation, however, things have changed. You have received the understanding you need to make your beliefs and convictions your own—to grow and mature in your own relationship with God.

Confirmation Promises for Girls has been designed to help you continue to grow and become established in your personal faith. Use it when you need to remember what the Bible says on a certain topic. Use it to memorize important verses that will strengthen and encourage you. And we've added devotional comments to some topics that we hope you will find helpful as you strive to become a godly woman.

Table of Contents

Learning is not attained by chance. It must be sought for with ardor and attended to with diligence.

ABIGAIL ADAMS

ASSURANCE

HEBREWS 11:1

Faith is being sure of what we hope for and certain of what we do not see.

ROMANS 8:38—39

I am convinced that neither death nor life, neither angels nor demons, neither the present nor the future, nor any powers, neither height nor depth, nor anything else in all creation, will be able to separate us from the love of God that is in Christ Jesus our Lord.

ISAIAH 54:10

"Though the mountains be shaken
    and the hills be removed,
    yet my unfailing love for you will not be shaken
nor my covenant of peace be removed,"
    says the LORD, who has compassion on you.

JOHN 10:27—29

Jesus said, "My sheep listen to my voice; I know them, and they follow me. I give them eternal life, and they shall never perish; no one can snatch

them out of my hand. My Father, who has given
them to me, is greater than all; no one can snatch
them out of my Father's hand."

I TIMOTHY 3:13
Those who have served well gain an excellent
standing and great assurance in their faith in
Christ Jesus.

2 TIMOTHY 1:12
I am not ashamed, because I know whom I have
believed, and am convinced that he is able to
guard what I have entrusted to him for that day.

HEBREWS 10:19, 22
Since we have confidence to enter the Most Holy
Place by the blood of Jesus ... let us draw near to
God with a sincere heart in full assurance of faith,
having our hearts sprinkled to cleanse us from a
guilty conscience and having our bodies washed
with pure water.

I JOHN 5:14 — 15
This is the confidence we have in approaching
God: that if we ask anything according to his will,
he hears us. And if we know that he hears us—
whatever we ask—we know that we have what we
asked of him.

Atonement

MATTHEW 26:28

Jesus said, "This is my blood of the covenant, which is poured out for many for the forgiveness of sins."

I JOHN 2:2

[Jesus Christ] is the atoning sacrifice for our sins, and not only for ours but also for the sins of the whole world.

COLOSSIANS 2:13—14

When you were dead in your sins and in the uncircumcision of your sinful nature, God made you alive with Christ. He forgave us all our sins, having canceled the written code, with its regulations, that was against us and that stood opposed to us; he took it away, nailing it to the cross.

HEBREWS 9:28

Christ was sacrificed once to take away the sins of many people; and he will appear a second time, not to bear sin, but to bring salvation to those who are waiting for him.

I JOHN 4:10

This is love: not that we loved God, but that he loved us and sent his Son as an atoning sacrifice for our sins.

ROMANS 5:9

Since we have now been justified by [Jesus'] blood, how much more shall we be saved from God's wrath through him!

I PETER 1:18—19

You know that it was not with perishable things such as silver or gold that you were redeemed from the empty way of life handed down to you from your forefathers, but with the precious blood of Christ, a lamb without blemish or defect.

COLOSSIANS 1:19—20

God was pleased to have all his fullness dwell in [Jesus], and through him to reconcile to himself all things, whether things on earth or things in heaven, by making peace through his blood, shed on the cross.

Baptism

I PETER 3:21

Water symbolizes baptism that now saves you also—not the removal of dirt from the body but the pledge of a good conscience toward God. It saves you by the resurrection of Jesus Christ.

LUKE 3:16

John answered them all, "I baptize you with water. But one more powerful than I will come, the thongs of whose sandals I am not worthy to untie. He will baptize you with the Holy Spirit and with fire."

EPHESIANS 4:4—6

There is one body and one Spirit— just as you were called to one hope when you were called— one Lord, one faith, one baptism; one God and Father of all, who is over all and through all and in all.

COLOSSIANS 2:11-12

In [Christ] you were also circumcised, in the putting off of the sinful nature, not with a circumcision done by the hands of men but with the circumcision done by Christ, having been buried with him in baptism and raised with him through your faith in the power of God, who raised him from the dead.

ROMANS 6:3 — 4

Don't you know that all of us who were baptized into Christ Jesus were baptized into his death? We were therefore buried with him through baptism into death in order that, just as Christ was raised from the dead through the glory of the Father, we too may live a new life.

JEREMIAH 33:8

I will cleanse them from all the sin they have committed against me and will forgive all their sins of rebellion against me.

HEBREWS 9:14

How much more, then, will the blood of Christ, who through the eternal Spirit offered himself unblemished to God, cleanse our consciences from acts that lead to death, so that we may serve the living God!

BEAUTY

PROVERBS 31:30

Charm is deceptive, and beauty is fleeting;
but a woman who fears the LORD is to
be praised.

GALATIANS 2:6

God does not judge by external appearance.

PSALM 139:13 — 14

You created my inmost being;
you knit me together in my mother's womb.
I praise you because I am fearfully and
wonderfully made;
your works are wonderful,
I know that full well.

I PETER 3:3 — 4

Your beauty should not come from outward
adornment, such as braided hair and the wearing
of gold jewelry and fine clothes. Instead, it
should be that of your inner self, the unfading
beauty of a gentle and quiet spirit, which is of
great worth in God's sight.

I SAMUEL 16:7

"The LORD does not look at the things man looks at. Man looks at the outward appearance, but the LORD looks at the heart."

MATTHEW 6:25

Jesus said, "Do not worry about your life, what you will eat or drink; or about your body, what you will wear. Is not life more important than food, and the body more important than clothes?"

I TIMOTHY 2:9—10

I also want women to dress modestly, with decency and propriety, not with braided hair or gold or pearls or expensive clothes, but with good deeds, appropriate for women who profess to worship God.

You Are So Beautiful!

If you covered the topic of beauty in your confirmation classes, you may have been surprised to learn that the Bible has so much to say about how you should dress. Maybe you were rolling your eyes—just a little—and whispering, "Yeah, right," when you read some of the verses. On the surface, it sounds like God is against braiding your hair—or that he wants you to buy all your clothes at a thrift shop (1 Timothy 2:9–10). What are you supposed to do—walk around looking all dull and drab?

Relax ... God isn't saying that it's a sin to wear pearls or gold jewelry. He isn't opposed to you finding your own unique style, whether that comes in the form of a totally awesome hairdo, great clothes, or fun "accessories." What he wants you to understand beyond a shadow of a doubt is that real beauty comes from within.

You see, in Bible times, some rich women made a habit of dressing up in fancy clothes to show how wealthy they were. They came to church looking very nice, but the part no one could see, their hearts, were ugly—haughty and filled with sin.

The point is that if you are longing to be noticed, to feel that you're someone special, it won't help to dye your hair pink or pierce your eyebrow or put on a pair of designer jeans. Those things just draw attention to how you look on the outside. The way to be noticed for who you are on the inside is to be kind to others and tenderhearted and respectful toward God. Those things reflect the inner beauty of a person who is becoming the woman God created her to be.

Make sure your outward appearance always reflects those things that are tucked deep inside—your values and commitments, and most of all, your relationship with God.

BELIEF

JOHN 3:16

Jesus said, "God so loved the world that he gave his one and only Son, that whoever believes in him shall not perish but have eternal life."

ROMANS 10:9 — 10

If you confess with your mouth, "Jesus is Lord," and believe in your heart that God raised him from the dead, you will be saved. For it is with your heart that you believe and are justified, and it is with your mouth that you confess and are saved.

ACTS 16:31

Believe in the Lord Jesus, and you will be saved—you and your household.

JOHN 6:47

Jesus said, "I tell you the truth, he who believes has everlasting life."

ACTS 10:43

All the prophets testify about [Jesus] that everyone
who believes in him receives forgiveness of sins
through his name.

JOHN 3:18

Jesus said, "Whoever believes in [the Son of God]
is not condemned."

JOHN 11:25 — 26

Jesus said to her, "I am the resurrection and the
life. He who believes in me will live, even though
he dies; and whoever lives and believes in me will
never die. Do you believe this?"

JOHN 1:12

To all who received [Jesus], to those who believed
in his name, he gave the right to become children
of God.

JOHN 20:29

Jesus told him, "Because you have seen me, you
have believed; blessed are those who have not
seen and yet have believed."

BIBLE STUDY

2 TIMOTHY 3:16 — 17

All Scripture is God-breathed and is useful for teaching, rebuking, correcting and training in righteousness, so that the man of God may be thoroughly equipped for every good work.

ROMANS 15:4

Everything that was written in the past was written to teach us, so that through endurance and the encouragement of the Scriptures we might have hope.

MATTHEW 4:4

Jesus answered, "It is written: 'Man does not live on bread alone, but on every word that comes from the mouth of God.'"

PSALM 119:165

Great peace have they who love your law,
    and nothing can make them stumble.

HEBREWS 4:12
The word of God is living and active. Sharper than any double-edged sword, it penetrates even to dividing soul and spirit, joints and marrow; it judges the thoughts and attitudes of the heart.

PSALM 119:105
Your word is a lamp to my feet
    and a light for my path.

DEUTERONOMY 7:12
If you pay attention to these laws and are careful to follow them, then the LORD your God will keep his covenant of love with you, as he swore to your forefathers.

PSALM 19:7
The law of the LORD is perfect,
    reviving the soul.
The statutes of the LORD are trustworthy,
    making wise the simple.

BLESSINGS

JEREMIAH 17:7

Blessed is the man who trusts in the LORD,
whose confidence is in him.

EPHESIANS 1:3

Praise be to the God and Father of our Lord Jesus
Christ, who has blessed us in the heavenly realms
with every spiritual blessing in Christ.

PSALM 1:1 — 2

Blessed is the man
who does not walk in the counsel of the wicked
or stand in the way of sinners
or sit in the seat of mockers.
But his delight is in the law of the LORD,
and on his law he meditates day and night.

JOHN 1:16

From the fullness of [God's] grace we have all
received one blessing after another.

PSALM 24:4—5

He who has clean hands and a pure heart,
who does not lift up his soul to an idol
or swear by what is false.
He will receive blessing from the LORD
and vindication from God his Savior.

LUKE 6:20—23

Looking at his disciples, Jesus said:
"Blessed are you who are poor,
for yours is the kingdom of God.
Blessed are you who hunger now,
for you will be satisfied.
Blessed are you who weep now,
for you will laugh.
Blessed are you when men hate you,
when they exclude you and insult you
and reject your name as evil,
because of the Son of Man.
Rejoice in that day and leap for joy, because
great is your reward in heaven."

BLOOD OF
JESUS

COLOSSIANS 1:19 — 20

God was pleased to have all his fullness dwell in [Jesus], and through him to reconcile to himself all things, whether things on earth or things in heaven, by making peace through his blood, shed on the cross.

1 JOHN 1:7

If we walk in the light, as [God] is in the light, we have fellowship with one another, and the blood of Jesus, his Son, purifies us from all sin.

MATTHEW 26:27 — 28

Jesus took the cup, gave thanks and offered it to [his disciples], saying, "Drink from it, all of you. This is my blood of the covenant, which is poured out for many for the forgiveness of sins."

EPHESIANS 2:13

In Christ Jesus you who once were far away have been brought near through the blood of Christ.

ROMANS 5:9

Since we have now been justified by [Jesus']
blood, how much more shall we be saved from
God's wrath through him!

COLOSSIANS 1:22

[God] has reconciled you by Christ's physical body
through death to present you holy in his sight,
without blemish and free from accusation.

I PETER 1:18 — 19

It was not with perishable things such as silver or
gold that you were redeemed from the empty way
of life handed down to you from your forefathers,
but with the precious blood of Christ, a lamb without blemish or defect.

BOLDNESS

ON YOUR CONFIRMATION

ISAIAH 50:7
> Because the Sovereign LORD helps me,
>> I will not be disgraced.
> Therefore have I set my face like flint,
>> and I know I will not be put to shame.

PROVERBS 28:1
> The wicked man flees though no one pursues,
>> but the righteous are as bold as a lion.

1 TIMOTHY 3:13
> Those who have served well gain an excellent standing and great assurance in their faith in Christ Jesus.

HEBREWS 13:6
> We say with confidence,
>> "The Lord is my helper; I will not be afraid.
>>> What can man do to me?"

JOSHUA 1:9

The LORD said to Joshua, "Have I not commanded
you? Be strong and courageous. Do not be
terrified; do not be discouraged, for the LORD your
God will be with you wherever you go."

HEBREWS 4:16

Let us then approach the throne of grace with
confidence, so that we may receive mercy and
find grace to help us in our time of need.

PSALM 138:3

When I called, O LORD, you answered me;
   you made me bold and stouthearted.

CHARACTER

I SAMUEL 16:7

"The LORD does not look at the things man looks
at. Man looks at the outward appearance, but the
LORD looks at the heart."

MATTHEW 5:6

Jesus said, "Blessed are those who hunger and
thirst for righteousness,
for they will be filled."

PROVERBS 5:21

A man's ways are in full view of the LORD,
and he examines all his paths.

ROMANS 5:3 — 5

We also rejoice in our sufferings, because we
know that suffering produces perseverance;
perseverance, character; and character, hope.
And hope does not disappoint us, because God
has poured out his love into our hearts by the
Holy Spirit, whom he has given us.

PROVERBS 16:17

The highway of the upright avoids evil;
   he who guards his way guards his life.

PSALM 119:1

Blessed are they whose ways are blameless,
   who walk according to the law of the LORD.

ISAIAH 32:8

The noble man makes noble plans,
   and by noble deeds he stands.

PROVERBS 22:1

A good name is more desirable than great riches;
   to be esteemed is better than silver or gold.

HEBREWS 10:23

Let us hold unswervingly to the hope we profess,
for [God] who promised is faithful.

1 CORINTHIANS 15:33

Do not be misled: "Bad company corrupts
good character."

Becoming a woman
of character

Character seems like a word for grown-ups, doesn't it? People who tell the truth, keep their promises, wouldn't think of taking something without paying for it—those people have character. You may have a sense that it also applies to grown-ups who live good lives in general and always care about doing the right thing. If this is what you think character is, you're right—all except for the part about it being just for grown-ups.

Proverbs 20:11 says, "Even a child is known by his actions, by whether his conduct is pure and right." Especially now that you have been confirmed into the Christian faith, you will be expected to live a life that exhibits good character.

That means you will want to carefully listen to your conscience, willingly obey your parents and teachers, and purposefully walk in the principles you learned in your confirmation class. It means considering the feelings of others, taking your responsibilities seriously—even in the little things like homework and chores—and refusing to take part in gossip. It will mean, in many cases, that you won't be able to go along with the crowd.

Character isn't about tallying up your good acts and bad acts. It's about consistently choosing to do those things that are pleasing to God. That will often place you in the uncomfortable position of saying "yes" when everyone around you is saying "no." Or saying "no" when everyone is saying "yes." You probably already know how tough that can be. But if you truly want to be a woman of character, you will have to get used to standing up and speaking out for what is right.

And there's one more thing. Most people who have good character don't suddenly develop it in adulthood. It is more often something that grows and matures with them. So now is the time to work on becoming a woman of good character. Begin by examining each choice that you face and asking yourself, *Will this thought or action be pleasing to God?*

CHARITY

LUKE 6:38

Jesus said, "Give, and it will be given to you. A good measure, pressed down, shaken together and running over, will be poured into your lap. For with the measure you use, it will be measured to you."

PROVERBS 14:21

Blessed is he who is kind to the needy.

PROVERBS 11:25

A generous man will prosper;
    he who refreshes others will himself
    be refreshed.

PROVERBS 28:27

He who gives to the poor will lack nothing.

2 CORINTHIANS 9:7

Each man should give what he has decided in his heart to give, not reluctantly or under compulsion, for God loves a cheerful giver.

MATTHEW 6:3 — 4

Jesus said, "When you give to the needy, do not let your left hand know what your right hand is doing, so that your giving may be in secret. Then your Father, who sees what is done in secret, will reward you."

DEUTERONOMY 15:7, 10

If there is a poor man among your brothers.... Give generously to him and do so without a grudging heart; then because of this the LORD your God will bless you in all your work and in everything you put your hand to.

MATTHEW 19:21

Jesus answered, "If you want to be perfect, go, sell your possessions and give to the poor, and you will have treasure in heaven. Then come, follow me."

1 CHRONICLES 29:14

But who am I, and who are my people, that we should be able to give as generously as this? Everything comes from you, and we have given you only what comes from your hand.

CHRIST'S RETURN

ACTS 1:11

"Men of Galilee," [the two men dressed in white] said, "why do you stand here looking into the sky? This same Jesus, who has been taken from you into heaven, will come back in the same way you have seen him go into heaven."

1 THESSALONIANS 4:16 — 17

The Lord himself will come down from heaven, with a loud command, with the voice of the archangel and with the trumpet call of God, and the dead in Christ will rise first. After that, we who are still alive and are left will be caught up together with them in the clouds to meet the Lord in the air. And so we will be with the Lord forever.

REVELATION 1:7

Look, he is coming with the clouds,
and every eye will see him.

JAMES 5:8

You too, be patient and stand firm, because the Lord's coming is near.

JOHN 14:2 — 3

Jesus said, "In my Father's house are many rooms; if it were not so, I would have told you. I am going there to prepare a place for you. And if I go and prepare a place for you, I will come back and take you to be with me that you also may be where I am."

LUKE 12:40

Jesus said, "You also must be ready, because the Son of Man will come at an hour when you do not expect him."

2 PETER 3:10

The day of the Lord will come like a thief. The heavens will disappear with a roar; the elements will be destroyed by fire, and the earth and everything in it will be laid bare.

MATTHEW 24:14

Jesus said, "This gospel of the kingdom will be preached in the whole world as a testimony to all nations, and then the end will come."

Jesus is coming!

Jesus' return for those who love him is the great hope of the Christian world. You may have heard about it from your parents or at church, and you almost certainly heard of it in your confirmation classes.

Adults often get real dreamy looks on their faces when they talk about that wonderful day. All their troubles gone for good. Living with the Lord forever. That's a lot to be happy about. At the same time, the idea of being "caught up" in the sky to meet Jesus in the air—oh, yeah, and without the slightest warning—would cause some anxious thoughts even for the most deeply committed Christian girl.

What if he comes while you're taking a bath or before you can put on an appropriate outfit? You probably wouldn't mind if he showed up in the middle of a big test, especially if you hadn't spent enough time studying, but what if it were prom day? Or graduation day? Or even your wedding day?

Have you ever prayed, *Lord, please don't come back until I have a chance to grow up, fall in love, get married, have a few kids, or at least, do something cool?* If so, don't worry. That's pretty normal.

The Bible says that no one knows the day or time when Jesus will return to gather his loved ones together and take them to be with him. That's pretty wise on God's part. Think about all the people who would be dumping their responsibilities and climbing up onto mountaintops to wait as the time drew near. On the other hand, many Christians would neglect their relationship with God if they knew his return was a long way off.

God hasn't disclosed the date of his return because he wants you to go on with your life—to live, to learn, to love, to laugh, to become all he created you to be. When he does come, will he find you doing what you are supposed to be doing—living your life for him?

CHURCH

I PETER 2:9

You are a chosen people, a royal priesthood, a holy nation, a people belonging to God, that you may declare the praises of him who called you out of darkness into his wonderful light.

I CORINTHIANS 12:12—13

The body is a unit, though it is made up of many parts; and though all its parts are many, they form one body. So it is with Christ. For we were all baptized by one Spirit into one body—whether Jews or Greeks, slave or free—and we were all given the one Spirit to drink.

I TIMOTHY 3:15

God's household...is the church of the living God, the pillar and foundation of the truth.

COLOSSIANS 1:18

Christ is the head of the body, the church; he is the beginning and the firstborn from among the dead, so that in everything he might have the supremacy.

I CORINTHIANS 12:27—28

You are the body of Christ, and each one of you is
a part of it. And in the church God has appointed
first of all apostles, second prophets, third
teachers, then workers of miracles, also those
having gifts of healing, those able to help others,
those with gifts of administration, and those
speaking in different kinds of tongues.

HEBREWS 10:25

Let us not give up meeting together, as some are
in the habit of doing, but let us encourage one
another—and all the more as you see the Day
approaching.

EPHESIANS 5:19—20

Speak to one another with psalms, hymns and
spiritual songs. Sing and make music in your heart
to the Lord, always giving thanks to God the
Father for everything, in the name of our Lord
Jesus Christ.

Commitment

I KINGS 8:61

Your hearts must be fully committed to the
LORD our God, to live by his decrees and obey
his commands, as at this time.

PSALM 37:5 — 6

Commit your way to the LORD;
    trust in him and he will do this:
He will make your righteousness
shine like the dawn
    the justice of your cause
    like the noonday sun.

PROVERBS 16:3

Commit to the LORD whatever you do,
    and your plans will succeed.

ECCLESIASTES 5:4

When you make a vow to God, do not delay
in fulfilling it.

PSALM 103:17—18

From everlasting to everlasting
the LORD's love is with those who fear him,
and his righteousness with their
children's children—
with those who keep his covenant
and remember to obey his precepts.

NUMBERS 30:2

When a man makes a vow to the LORD or takes an
oath to obligate himself by a pledge, he must not
break his word but must do everything he said.

2 CHRONICLES 16:9

The eyes of the LORD range throughout the earth to
strengthen those whose hearts are fully committed
to him.

PSALM 22:25

From you comes the theme of my praise in the
great assembly; before
those who fear you will I fulfill my vows.

DEUTERONOMY 6:25

And if we are careful to obey all this law before
the LORD our God, as he has commanded us, that
will be our righteousness.

Communication

PROVERBS 18:20

From the fruit of his mouth a man's stomach
is filled;
    with the harvest from his lips he is satisfied.

PROVERBS 13:3

He who guards his lips guards his life.
    But he who speaks rashly will come to ruin.

PSALM 37:30 — 31

The mouth of the righteous man utters wisdom,
    and his tongue speaks what is just.
The law of his God is in his heart;
    his feet do not slip.

PROVERBS 10:19 — 20

He who holds his tongue is wise.
The tongue of the righteous is choice silver.

PROVERBS 13:2

From the fruit of his lips a man enjoys

good things.

EPHESIANS 4:15

Speaking the truth in love, we will in all things
grow up into him who is the Head, that is, Christ.

PSALM 19:14

May the words of my mouth and the meditation
of my heart
    be pleasing in your sight,
        O LORD, my Rock and my Redeemer.

1 PETER 3:15-16

Always be prepared to give an answer to everyone
who asks you to give the reason for the hope that
you have. But do this with gentleness and respect,
keeping a clear conscience, so that those who
speak maliciously against your good behavior in
Christ may be ashamed of their slander.

The gift of gab

Girls love to talk. And they're good at it. It must just be part of their genetic makeup. Sure, some are shier and less verbal, but for the most part, girls are blessed with the gift of gab. That's why it's so important to form good communication habits at an early age.

In your confirmation classes, you were most likely encouraged to avoid gossip and lying, cursing and disrespect. Those are the negative aspects of communication. You've probably heard enough about those. But what about the positive aspects of communication? Does the Bible mention the good your words can do? Of course it does.

For one thing, the Bible says that words have power. God used them to create the universe—"Let there be light!" followed by, "Let there be 'this,'" and, "Let there be 'that,'" until every single thing was set in place. Jesus used his words to heal; "Receive your sight," he said to the blind man. He used his words to forgive; "Your sins are forgiven," he said to the paralyzed man. He used his words to restore life; "My child, get up!" he said to the girl who died before her father could bring Jesus to heal her.

Your words may not be powerful to the extent that Jesus' words were, but they do pack a punch. They can create a new sense of hope in a person who is discouraged. They can mend broken relationships. They can inspire love and courage and faith.

In addition to being powerful, words are eternal. Some physicists believe that sound waves keep going right out into space and then on and on forever. That means your words never disappear; they just travel away from you. Who knows if that is true—even scientists aren't sure. But you can be certain that at least some of your words are recorded in heaven—words of repentance and words of worship. And like the words of Jesus, your words can change someone's life.

Learning to respect your words and use them wisely is one of the most important steps you can take toward becoming a godly woman. That doesn't mean that you can't enjoy hours of friendly chatter. Just be careful that all your words are pleasing to God.

Communion

I CORINTHIANS 10:16 — 17

Is not the cup of thanksgiving for which we give thanks a participation in the blood of Christ? And is not the bread that we break a participation in the body of Christ? Because there is one loaf, we, who are many, are one body, for we all partake of the one loaf.

MATTHEW 26:27 — 29

[Jesus] took the cup, gave thanks and offered it to them, saying, "Drink from it, all of you. This is my blood of the covenant, which is poured out for many for the forgiveness of sins. I tell you, I will not drink of this fruit of the vine from now on until that day when I drink it anew with you in my Father's kingdom."

LUKE 22:14-16

When the hour came, Jesus and his apostles reclined at the table. And he said to them, "I have eagerly desired to eat this Passover with you before I suffer. For I tell you, I will not eat it again until it finds fulfillment in the kingdom of God."

JOHN 6:53 — 54

Jesus said to them, "I tell you the truth, unless you eat the flesh of the Son of Man and drink his blood, you have no life in you. Whoever eats my flesh and drinks my blood has eternal life, and I will raise him up at the last day."

LUKE 22:19 — 20

[Jesus] took bread, gave thanks and broke it, and gave it to [his apostles], saying, "This is my body given for you; do this in remembrance of me."

In the same way, after the supper he took the cup, saying, "This cup is the new covenant in my blood, which is poured out for you."

I CORINTHIANS 11:26

Whenever you eat this bread and drink this cup, you proclaim the Lord's death until he comes.

Compassion

PSALM 119:77

Let your compassion come to me that I may live,
for your law is my delight.

EPHESIANS 4:32 — 5:2

Be kind and compassionate to one another,
forgiving each other, just as in Christ God forgave you. Be imitators of God, therefore, as
dearly loved children and live a life of love, just
as Christ loved us and gave himself up for us as
a fragrant offering and sacrifice to God.

ISAIAH 30:18

The LORD longs to be gracious to you;
he rises to show you compassion.
For the LORD is a God of justice.
Blessed are all who wait for him!

ISAIAH 54:10

"Though the mountains be shaken
and the hills be removed,

yet my unfailing love for you will not be shaken
nor my covenant of peace be removed,"
says the LORD, who has compassion on you.

PSALM 86:15

You, O LORD, are a compassionate and
gracious God,
slow to anger, abounding in love
and faithfulness.

HOSEA 2:19

"I will betroth you to me forever;
I will betroth you in righteousness and justice,
in love and compassion,"
declares the LORD.

PSALM 145:9

The LORD is good to all;
he has compassion on all he has made.

MATTHEW 10:42

Jesus said, "And if anyone gives even a cup of cold
water to one of these little ones because he is my
disciple, I tell you the truth, he will certainly not
lose his reward."

Contentment

HEBREWS 13:5

Keep your lives free from the love of money and be content with what you have, because God has said,

"Never will I leave you;
never will I forsake you."

PROVERBS 16:8

Better a little with righteousness
than much gain with injustice.

PHILIPPIANS 4:11 — 13

I have learned to be content whatever the circumstances. I know what it is to be in need, and I know what it is to have plenty. I have learned the secret of being content in any and every situation, whether well fed or hungry, whether living in plenty or in want. I can do everything through him who gives me strength.

I TIMOTHY 6:6 — 8

Godliness with contentment is great gain. For we brought nothing into the world, and we can take nothing out of it. If we have food and clothing, we will be content with that.

PSALM 37:16 — 17

Better the little that the righteous have
  than the wealth of many wicked;
for the power of the wicked will be broken,
  but the LORD upholds the righteous.

PROVERBS 19:23

The fear of the LORD leads to life:
  Then one rests content, untouched by trouble.

ECCLESIASTES 4:6

Better one handful with tranquility
  than two handfuls with toil
  and chasing after the wind.

PSALM 23:1 — 3

The LORD is my shepherd, I shall not be in want.
He makes me lie down in green pastures,
  he leads me beside quiet waters,
  he restores my soul.
He guides me in paths of righteousness
  for his name's sake.

DECISION
MAKING

HAGGAI 1:5
This is what the LORD Almighty says: "Give careful thought to your ways."

PROVERBS 3:21—24
Preserve sound judgment and discernment,
    do not let them out of your sight;
they will be life for you,
    an ornament to grace your neck.
Then you will go on your way in safety,
    and your foot will not stumble;
when you lie down, you will not be afraid;
    when you lie down, your sleep will be sweet.

PSALM 37:5—6
Commit your way to the LORD;
    trust in him and he will do this:
He will make your righteousness shine
like the dawn,
    the justice of your cause like the noonday sun.

I CORINTHIANS 2:16

Who has known the mind of the Lord that he may instruct him? But we have the mind of Christ.

JAMES 1:5

If any of you lacks wisdom, he should ask God, who gives generously to all without finding fault, and it will be given to him.

PROVERBS 3:5 — 6

Trust in the LORD with all your heart
    and lean not on your own understanding;
in all your ways acknowledge him,
    and he will make your paths straight.

JOHN 14:16 — 17

Jesus said, "I will ask the Father, and he will give you another Counselor to be with you forever— the Spirit of truth. The world cannot accept him, because it neither sees him nor knows him. But you know him, for he lives with you and will be in you."

DEFENDING THE WEAK

MATTHEW 10:42

Jesus said, "If anyone gives even a cup of cold water to one of these little ones because he is my disciple, I tell you the truth, he will certainly not lose his reward."

ROMANS 15:1

We who are strong ought to bear with the failings of the weak and not to please ourselves.

ISAIAH 1:17

Learn to do right!
Seek justice,
    encourage the oppressed.
Defend the cause of the fatherless,
    plead the case of the widow.

I THESSALONIANS 5:14

We urge you, brothers, warn those who are idle, encourage the timid, help the weak, be patient with everyone.

MATTHEW 25:35—40

Jesus said, "I was hungry and you gave me something to eat, I was thirsty and you gave me something to drink, I was a stranger and you invited
me in, I needed clothes and you clothed me, I
was sick and you looked after me, I was in prison
and you came to visit me. Then the righteous will
answer him, 'Lord, when did we see you hungry
and feed you, or thirsty and give you something
to drink? When did we see you a stranger and
invite you in, or needing clothes and clothe you?
When did we see you sick or in prison and go to
visit you?' The King will reply, I tell you the
truth, whatever you did for one of the least of
these brothers of mine, you did for me."

PROVERBS 29:7

The righteous care about justice for the poor,
    but the wicked have no such concern.

PROVERBS 31:8—9

Speak up for those who cannot speak
for themselves,
    for the rights of all who are destitute.
Speak up and judge fairly;
    defend the rights of the poor and needy.

Devotion to God

MATTHEW 6:24

Jesus said, "No one can serve two masters. Either he will hate the one and love the other, or he will be devoted to the one and despise the other. You cannot serve both God and Money."

I CHRONICLES 28:9

Acknowledge the God of your father, and serve him with wholehearted devotion and with a willing mind, for the LORD searches every heart and understands every motive behind the thoughts. If you seek him, he will be found by you.

MATTHEW 22:37—38

Jesus replied: "'Love the Lord your God with all your heart and with all your soul and with all your mind.' This is the first and greatest commandment."

PSALM 141:8

My eyes are fixed on you, O Sovereign LORD;
in you I take refuge.

DEUTERONOMY 6:5

Love the LORD your God with all your heart and
with all your soul and with all your strength.

PSALM 86:2

Guard my life, for I am devoted to you.
    You are my God; save your servant
    who trusts in you.

JOB 11:13, 15, 18

"If you devote your heart to him
    and stretch out your hands to him,
then you will lift up your face without shame;
    you will stand firm and without fear.
You will be secure, because there is hope;
    you will look about you and take your rest
    in safety."

PSALM 63:1—3

O God, you are my God,
    earnestly I seek you;
my soul thirsts for you,
    my body longs for you,
in a dry and weary land
    where there is no water.
I have seen you in the sanctuary
    and beheld your power and your glory.
Because your love is better than life,
    my lips will glorify you.

Discernment

PROVERBS 10:13

Wisdom is found on the lips of the discerning.

I KINGS 3:9 — 10

Solomon prayed to the LORD, "Give your servant a discerning heart to govern your people and to distinguish between right and wrong. For who is able to govern this great people of yours?"

The Lord was pleased that Solomon had asked for this.

ECCLESIASTES 8:5

Whoever obeys [the King's] command will come to no harm,
and the wise heart will know the proper time and procedure.

PROVERBS 15:21

Folly delights a man who lacks judgment,
but a man of understanding keeps a straight course.

PHILIPPIANS 1:9-11

This is my prayer: that your love may abound more and more in knowledge and depth of insight, so you will be able to discern what is best and may be pure and blameless until the day of Christ, filled with the fruit of righteousness that comes through Jesus Christ—to the glory and praise of God.

2 TIMOTHY 2:7

Reflect on what I am saying, for the Lord will give you insight into all this.

1 JOHN 4:6

We are from God, and whoever knows God listens to us; but whoever is not from God does not listen to us. This is how we recognize the Spirit of truth and the spirit of falsehood.

ROMANS 12:1

Do not conform any longer to the pattern of this world, but be transformed by the renewing of your mind. Then you will be able to test and approve what God's will is—his good, pleasing and perfect will.

DISCIPLESHIP

JOHN 12:26

Jesus said, "Whoever serves me must follow me; and where I am, my servant also will be. My Father will honor the one who serves me."

MATTHEW 16:24 — 25

Jesus said to his disciples, "If anyone would come after me, he must deny himself and take up his cross and follow me. For whoever wants to save his life will lose it, but whoever loses his life for me will find it."

JOHN 8:12

Jesus said, "I am the light of the world. Whoever follows me will never walk in darkness, but will have the light of life."

JOHN 8:31-32

To the Jews who had believed him, Jesus said, "If you hold to my teaching, you are really my disciples. Then you will know the truth and the truth will set you free."

JOHN 14:21

Jesus said, "Whoever has my commands and obeys them, he is the one who loves me. He who loves me will be loved by my Father, and I too will love him and show myself to him."

MATTHEW 28:18—20

Jesus came to [his disciples] and said, "All authority in heaven and on earth has been given to me. Therefore go and make disciples of all nations, baptizing them in the name of the Father and of the Son and of the Holy Spirit, and teaching them to obey everything I have commanded you. And surely I am with you to the very end of the age."

JOHN 15:8

Jesus said, "This is to my Father's glory, that you bear much fruit, showing yourselves to be my disciples."

JOHN 13:35

Jesus said, "By this all men will know that you are my disciples, if you love one another."

ETERNAL LIFE

JOHN 3:16

Jesus said, "God so loved the world that he gave his one and only Son, that whoever believes in him shall not perish but have eternal life."

I JOHN 5:11—12

This is the testimony: God has given us eternal life, and this life is in his Son. He who has the Son has life; he who does not have the Son of God does not have life.

JOHN 17:3

Jesus prayed, "This is eternal life: that they may know you, the only true God, and Jesus Christ, whom you have sent."

ROMANS 6:23

The wages of sin is death, but the gift of God is eternal life in Christ Jesus our Lord.

JOHN 3:36

Whoever believes in the Son has eternal life.

TITUS 3:7

Having been justified by his grace, we might
become heirs having the hope of eternal life.

JOHN 11:25 — 26

Jesus said [to Martha], "I am the resurrection and
the life. He who believes in me will live, even
though he dies; and whoever lives and believes in
me will never die. Do you believe this?"

JOHN 10:27 — 29

Jesus said, "My sheep listen to my voice; I know
them, and they follow me. I give them eternal life,
and they shall never perish; no one can snatch
them out of my hand. My Father, who has given
them to me, is greater than all; no one can snatch
them out of my Father's hand."

Evangelism

1 PETER 3:15

In your hearts set apart Christ as Lord. Always be prepared to give an answer to everyone who asks you to give the reason for the hope that you have. But do this with gentleness and respect.

MATTHEW 28:19—20

Jesus said, "Therefore go and make disciples of all nations, baptizing them in the name of the Father and of the Son and of the Holy Spirit, and teaching them to obey everything I have commanded you. And surely I am with you always, to the very end of the age."

1 CHRONICLES 16:8—9

Give thanks to the Lord, call on his name;
    make known among the nations what he
    has done.
Sing to him, sing praise to him;
    tell of all his wonderful acts.

PHILEMON 1:6

I pray that you may be active in sharing your faith, so that you will have a full understanding of every good thing we have in Christ.

JOHN 20:21

Jesus said, "Peace be with you! As the Father has sent me, I am sending you."

LUKE 8:16

Jesus said, "No one lights a lamp and hides it in a jar or puts it under a bed. Instead, he puts it on a stand, so that those who come in can see the light."

MATTHEW 10:32

Jesus said, "Whoever acknowledges me before men, I will also acknowledge him before my Father in heaven."

ROMANS 1:16

I am not ashamed of the gospel, because it is the power of God for the salvation of everyone who believes.

PROMISES FOR GIRLS

Faith

PSALM 40:4

Blessed is the man
   who makes the LORD his trust,
who does not look to the proud,
   to those who turn aside to false gods.

EPHESIANS 6:16

Take up the shield of faith, with which you can
extinguish all the flaming arrows of the evil one.

PSALM 112:1, 7—8

Blessed is the man who fears the LORD,
   who finds great delight in his commands....
He will have no fear of bad news;
   his heart is steadfast, trusting in the LORD.
His heart is secure, he will have no fear;
   in the end he will look in triumph on his foes.

1 TIMOTHY 6:11

Pursue righteousness, godliness, faith, love,
endurance and gentleness.

PSALM 20:7

Some trust in chariots and some in horses,
   but we trust in the name of the LORD our God.

MATTHEW 21:21

Jesus replied, "I tell you the truth, if you have
faith and do not doubt, not only can you do what
was done to the fig tree, but also you can say to
this mountain, 'Go, throw yourself into the sea,'
and it will be done."

1 PETER 1:21

Through [Christ] you believe in God, who raised
him from the dead and glorified him, and so your
faith and hope are in God.

HEBREWS 11:1

Now faith is being sure of what we hope for and
certain of what we do not see.

MATTHEW 17:20

Jesus replied, "Because you have so little faith. I
tell you the truth, if you have faith as small as a
mustard seed, you can say to this mountain, 'Move
from here to there' and it will move. Nothing will
be impossible for you."

Family

GALATIANS 3:29

If you belong to Christ, then you are Abraham's seed, and heirs according to the promise.

DEUTERONOMY 5:16

"Honor your father and your mother, as the LORD your God has commanded you, so that you may live long and that it may go well with you in the land the LORD your God is giving you," says the LORD.

HEBREWS 2:11

Both the one who makes men holy and those who are made holy are of the same family. So Jesus is not ashamed to call them brothers.

1 JOHN 3:1

How great is the love the Father has lavished on us, that we should be called children of God! And that is what we are!

PSALM 68:6

God sets the lonely in families.

I TIMOTHY 5:4

If a widow has children or grandchildren, these should learn first of all to put their religion into practice by caring for their own family and so repaying their parents and grandparents, for this is pleasing to God.

PROVERBS 17:6

Children's children are a crown to the aged,
   and parents are the pride of their children.

GALATIANS 6:10

As we have opportunity, let us do good to all people, especially to those who belong to the family of believers.

ROMANS 8:16

The Spirit himself testifies with our spirit that we are God's children.

I JOHN 3:2

Dear friends, now we are children of God, and what we will be has not yet been made known. But we know that when he appears, we shall be like him, for we shall see him as he is.

families are forever

If you are like most girls your age, there are times when you wonder how you ended up in a family full of freaks! Maybe it's your dad breaking into his Elton John impersonation right in front of your friends. Or your mom giving you the third degree every time you go out the door. Do you have brothers and sisters? You adore each other, right? The crazy thing is that one day, not so long from now, your family—the one with all those people who are about to get on your last nerve—will become your closest friends on earth.

That's the way it works. When you grow up and leave home, you begin to see your family in a different light. Dad's impersonations strike you as funny and endearing rather than embarrassing. You begin to see that your mom's constant questioning was intended to keep you safe. And those brothers and sisters? No one understands you as much as someone who grew up in the same family with you.

God created the human family way back in the Garden of Eden. And he uses the concept of family to teach us how we are to live together as Christians here on earth. Do we always like other Christians? You can probably name at least a few who drive you crazy. You see, like your human family, your Christian brothers and sisters are also in the process of growing up. There they are, acting weird, getting on your nerves—and yet, God goes right on expecting you to love them.

Your father and mother, brothers and sisters are a gift to you from God. If you can't embrace that thought quite yet, at least know that the day is coming when you will. And that other family— the family of God—is also a gift to you. One day we will all live together in heaven, so start learning to appreciate each other now.

FELLOWSHIP

MATTHEW 18:20

Jesus said, "Where two or three come together in my name, there am I with them."

I JOHN 1:7

If we walk in the light, as Christ is in the light, we have fellowship with one another.

I PETER 3:8—9

Live in harmony with one another; be sympathetic, love as brothers, be compassionate and humble. Do not repay evil with evil or insult with insult, but with blessing, because to this you were called so that you may inherit a blessing.

PHILIPPIANS 2:3—4

In humility consider others better than yourselves. Each of you should look not only to your own interests, but also to the interests of others.

ROMANS 14:19

Let us therefore make every effort to do what
leads to peace and to mutual edification.

COLOSSIANS 3:16

Let the word of Christ dwell in you richly as you
teach and admonish one another with all wisdom,
and as you sing psalms, hymns and spiritual songs
with gratitude in your hearts to God.

PSALM 133

How good and pleasant it is
    when brothers live together in unity!
It is like precious oil poured on the head,
    running down on the beard,
running down on Aaron's beard,
    down upon the collar of his robes.
It is as if the dew of Hermon
    were falling on Mount Zion.
For there the LORD bestows his blessing,
    even life forevermore.

FORGIVENESS

I JOHN 1:9
If we confess our sins, he is faithful and just
and will forgive us our sins and purify us from
all unrighteousness.

ROMANS 4:8
Blessed is the man whose sin the Lord will never
count against him.

PROVERBS 25:21 — 22
If your enemy is hungry, give him food to eat;
    if he is thirsty, give him water to drink.
In doing this, you will heap burning coals on
his head,
    and the LORD will reward you.

MATTHEW 6:14 — 15
Jesus said, "If you forgive men when they sin
against you, your heavenly Father will also
forgive you. But if you do not forgive men their
sins, your Father will not forgive your sins."

COLOSSIANS 3:13—14

Bear with each other and forgive whatever
grievances you may have against one another.
Forgive as the Lord forgave you. And over all
these virtues put on love, which binds them all
together in perfect unity.

ISAIAH 43:25

This is what the LORD says,
  "I, even I, am he who blots out
    your transgressions, for my own sake,
    and remembers your sins no more."

PSALM 103:12

As far as the east is from the west,
  so far has he removed our transgressions
    from us.

MICAH 7:18

Who is a God like you,
  who pardons sin and forgives the
    transgression
  of the remnant of his inheritance?
You do not stay angry forever
  but delight to show mercy.

FRiENDSHiP

PROVERBS 27:6

Wounds from a friend can be trusted.

ROMANS 12:10

Be devoted to one another in brotherly love.
Honor one another above yourselves.

PROVERBS 17:17

A friend loves at all times,
    and a brother is born for adversity.

JOHN 15:13 — 15

Jesus said, "Greater love has no one than this,
that he lay down his life for his friends. You are
my friends if you do what I command. I no
longer call you servants, because a servant does
not know his master's business. Instead, I have
called you friends, for everything that I learned
from my Father I have made known to you."

PROVERBS 18:24

A man of many companions may come to ruin,
but there is a friend who sticks closer than
a brother.

PROVERBS 27:10

Do not forsake your friend and the friend of
your father.

ECCLESIASTES 4:9—12

Two are better than one,
because they have a good return
for their work:
If one falls down,
his friend can help him up.
But pity the man who falls
and has no one to help him up!
Also, if two lie down together, they will
keep warm.
But how can one keep warm alone?
Though one may be overpowered,
two can defend themselves.
A cord of three strands is not quickly broken.

PROVERBS 27:17

As iron sharpens iron,
so one man sharpens another.

The gift of friendship

Good friends are treasures; they're worth making and worth keeping. Time spent with "best buds," even watching a movie or being silly together, is like a little slice of heaven. Friends see the good, the bad, and the not-so-pretty—and yet, they continue to love you.

As you move into your teenage years, the idea of friendship can get confusing. Boys start to enter the picture more often. Life becomes a bit more complicated. You may feel pressures at school that cloud your thoughts about which people would make the best friends. At these times, it's more important than ever to have friends who build you up and share the same convictions.

When it comes to making new friends, it's natural for you to be drawn together by mutual interests, like soccer, music, or art. But, as you get to know each other better, you see the deeper traits. These are the elements in friendship that really count—things like trust, encouragement, and forgiveness.

No friendship can survive without trust. Girls have thoughts or dreams that they want to talk about with their friends. Some might be considered "secrets." It's valuable to be able to share your heart with a friend and know that your friend will guard it. Be a friend who's trustworthy, and be careful to reserve your deepest thoughts for friends who are true confidants.

One of the greatest gifts of friendship is encouragement. The Bible says, "If one falls down, his friend can help him up" (Ecclesiastes 4:10). When your day has "bad" written all over it in red ink, you want a friend you can talk with, someone who won't mind if you download every detail of your day—or even shed a few tears. Sometimes the best encouragement is simply being there and listening.

No friendship is perfect, because all human beings have flaws. You will offend your friends, even if you don't mean to. Your friends will hurt you. When you've had a conflict, it's good to get things out in the open and talk them through. When the talking is done, forgive your friend. And don't be afraid to tell a friend, with tact and love, if you think she's doing something that could hurt her or someone else. Friends look out for one another, pray for each other, and speak the truth to each other.

And if you're still looking for a "best" friend, talk to God about that. You will find, as so many people already have, that God can be the best Friend of all!

GOD'S LOVE

1 JOHN 4:9—10

This is how God showed his love among us: He
sent his one and only Son into the world that we
might live through him. This is love: not that we
loved God, but that he loved us and sent his Son
as an atoning sacrifice for our sins.

PSALM 103:11

As high as the heavens are above the earth,
so great is God's love for those who fear him.

JOHN 14:21

Jesus replied, "He who loves me will be loved by
my Father, and I too will love him and show
myself to him."

ROMANS 5:8

God demonstrates his own love for us in this:
While we were still sinners, Christ died for us.

I JOHN 4:16 — 17

God is love. Whoever lives in love lives in God, and God in him. In this way, love is made complete among us so that we will have confidence on the day of judgment, because in this world we are like him.

PSALM 103:17

From everlasting to everlasting
    the LORD's love is with those who fear him,
    and his righteousness with their
    children's children.

I JOHN 3:16

This is how we know what love is: Jesus Christ laid down his life for us. And we ought to lay down our lives for our brothers.

PSALM 32:10

Many are the woes of the wicked,
    but the LORD's unfailing love
    surrounds the man who trusts in him.

Never-Ending Love

"God loves you." That's probably one of the first things you learned in confirmation class. You may have even accepted that as a fact. But how can you really know that it's true?

We can't always feel God's love, but God has shown us countless ways that he loves us beyond anything we can fathom or measure. First, the Bible tells us that God created us—and not only that, but he made us so that we could be his friends. When Adam and Eve committed the first sin in the Garden of Eden, they turned away from God. Yet he never stopped loving them. He even kept right on loving their children and their children's children and their children's children's children—all the way down to you and your whole generation.

Not only did God keep on loving, but he loved so deeply and strongly that he made a provision that would allow him to forgive Adam and Eve's sin and keep you—and all who came before and after you—in fellowship with him. God sent his only Son, Jesus, to live as a man and die on the cross to pay for your sins. It's like God chose to forgive you in advance for anything you might ever do. You can never do anything bad enough to forfeit God's love.

What a comfort and privilege to know as you walk through life that your heavenly Father cares so deeply for you. When times are good, you can know that there is Someone nearby who is celebrating with you. When times are bad, you can rest assured, knowing that you aren't alone. God is as close as the breath on your cheek. When you feel left out, rejected, friendless, or hopeless, God is there. His love is enough to counteract a billion bad feelings. All you have to do is reach out and take it.

GOD'S WILL

1 JOHN 2:17

The world and its desires pass away, but the man who does the will of God lives forever.

ROMANS 12:2

Do not conform any longer to the pattern of this world, but be transformed by the renewing of your mind. Then you will be able to test and approve what God's will is—his good, pleasing and perfect will.

EPHESIANS 1:9—10

[God] made known to us the mystery of his will according to his good pleasure, which he purposed in Christ, to be put into effect when the times will have reached their fulfillment—to bring all things in heaven and on earth together under one head, even Christ.

I THESSALONIANS 5:16—18

Be joyful always; pray continually; give thanks in all circumstances, for this is God's will for you in Christ Jesus.

EPHESIANS 1:11—12

In [Christ] we were also chosen, having been predestined according to the plan of him who works out everything in conformity with the purpose of his will, in order that we, who were the first to hope in Christ, might be for the praise of his glory.

JOHN 6:40

Jesus said, "My Father's will is that everyone who looks to the Son and believes in him shall have eternal life, and I will raise him up at the last day."

HEBREWS 10:36

You need to persevere so that when you have done the will of God, you will receive what he has promised.

GOD'S WORD

MARK 13:31
Jesus said, "Heaven and earth will pass away, but my words will never pass away."

HEBREWS 4:12
The word of God is living and active. Sharper than any double-edged sword, it penetrates even to dividing soul and spirit, joints and marrow; it judges the thoughts and attitudes of the heart.

2 TIMOTHY 3:16 — 17
All Scripture is God-breathed and is useful for teaching, rebuking, correcting and training in righteousness, so that the man of God may be thoroughly equipped for every good work.

JOSHUA 1:8
"Do not let this Book of the Law depart from your mouth; meditate on it day and night, so that you may be careful to do everything written in it. Then you will be prosperous and successful," says the LORD.

PSALM 119:105

Your word is a lamp to my feet
and a light for my path.

MATTHEW 4:4

Jesus answered, "It is written: 'Man does not live
on bread alone, but on every word that comes
from the mouth of God.'"

PSALM 119:11

I have hidden your word in my heart
that I might not sin against you.

LUKE 11:28

Jesus replied, "Blessed rather are those who hear
the word of God and obey it."

ISAIAH 55:11

So is my word that goes out from my mouth:
It will not return to me empty,
but will accomplish what I desire
and achieve the purpose for which I sent it.

Living words

Have you ever found yourself captivated by a good book? The words follow you around during the day and visit your dreams at night. They enliven the characters as they describe what they say and what they do. The words in some books can even influence your whole way of looking at life. Books are powerful because of the words they contain. And we're talking about books written by human writers. Imagine how powerful a book would be if it were written by God.

Second Timothy 3:16–17 says that the Bible is "God-breathed." It was written as God placed his words into the minds and hearts of many different people and used their hands to record them on paper.

Inside the pages of God's Word—the Bible— you will find exciting stories of love, mystery, and mighty miracles. There are poems, songs, and wise words written by kings. When you read the Gospels, you can walk with Christ as he lived on earth and become part of the crowds listening to his teaching. The Bible is filled with the history of God's love for you. Reading the Bible is like sitting down and talking to God face to face. If ever a book were captivating, this one is.

However, knowing that the Bible is God's living Word doesn't necessarily make it any easier for you to open the cover. It's the Good Book—but it's still a mighty big book! Try not to get overwhelmed. Books that have a short reading for each day are perfect for people who have a lot going on in their lives (like you!). There are "study" Bibles and Bible studies especially for people around your age. One of the best ways to study the Bible is with a group of friends.

What's important is to try to make God's Word, if only a couple verses, part of your life every day. God's Word, the Bible, is the most powerful book of all—plug into it!

GRACE

2 CORINTHIANS 9:8

God is able to make all grace abound to you, so
that in all things at all times, having all that you
need, you will abound in every good work.

EPHESIANS 2:4—5

Because of his great love for us, God, who is rich
in mercy, made us alive with Christ even when
we were dead in transgressions—it is by grace
you have been saved.

2 TIMOTHY 1:9

[God] has saved us and called us to a holy life—
not because of anything we have done but
because of his own purpose and grace. This grace
was given us in Christ Jesus before the beginning
of time.

PSALM 145:8

The LORD is gracious and compassionate,
    slow to anger and rich in love.

EPHESIANS 2:8—10

It is by grace you have been saved, through faith—
and this not from yourselves, it is the gift of God—
not by works, so that no one can boast. For we
are God's workmanship, created in Christ Jesus to
do good works, which God prepared in advance
for us to do.

JAMES 4:6

[God] gives us more grace. That is why
Scripture says:

"God opposes the proud
but gives grace to the humble."

2 CORINTHIANS 8:9

You know the grace of our Lord Jesus Christ, that
though he was rich, yet for your sakes he became
poor, so that you through his poverty might
become rich.

HEAVEN

REVELATION 22:3—5

No longer will there be any curse. The throne of God and of the Lamb will be in the city, and his servants will serve him. They will see his face, and his name will be on their foreheads. There will be no more night. They will not need the light of a lamp or the light of the sun, for the Lord God will give them light. And they will reign for ever and ever.

REVELATION 22:14

Jesus said, "Blessed are those who wash their robes, that they may have the right to the tree of life and may go through the gates into the city."

PHILIPPIANS 3:20—21

Our citizenship is in heaven. And we eagerly await a Savior from there, the Lord Jesus Christ. God who, by the power that enables him to bring everything under his control, will transform our lowly bodies so that they will be like his glorious body.

REVELATION 21:4

[God] will wipe every tear from their eyes.
There will be no more death or mourning or
crying or pain, for the old order of things has
passed away.

JOHN 14:2 — 3

Jesus said, "In my Father's house are many
rooms; if it were not so, I would have told you.
I am going there to prepare a place for you."
Jesus said, "If I go and prepare a place for you, I
will come back and take you to be with me that
you also may be where I am."

HOLY SPIRIT

1 JOHN 4:1—2

Do not believe every spirit, but test the spirits to see whether they are from God.... This is how you can recognize the Spirit of God: Every spirit that acknowledges that Jesus Christ has come in the flesh is from God.

2 CORINTHIANS 3:17

The Lord is the Spirit, and where the Spirit of the Lord is, there is freedom.

JOHN 14:16—17

Jesus said, "I will ask the Father, and he will give you another Counselor to be with you forever—the Spirit of truth. The world cannot accept him, because it neither sees him nor knows him. But you know him, for he lives with you and will be in you."

ACTS 2:38—39

Peter replied, "Repent and be baptized, every one of you, in the name of Jesus Christ for the forgiveness of your sins. And you will receive the gift of the Holy Spirit. The promise is for you and your children and for all who are far off—for all whom the Lord our God will call."

ROMANS 8:26—27

In the same way, the Spirit helps us in our weakness. We do not know what we ought to pray for, but the Spirit himself intercedes for us with groans that words cannot express. And he who searches our hearts knows the mind of the Spirit, because the Spirit intercedes for the saints in accordance with God's will.

JOB 33:4

The Spirit of God has made me;
    the breath of the Almighty gives me life.

ISAIAH 44:3

For I will pour water on the thirsty land,
    and streams on the dry ground;
I will pour out my Spirit on your offspring,
    and my blessing on your descendants.

HOSPITALITY

I PETER 4:9
Offer hospitality to one another without grumbling.

TITUS I:8
[An overseer] must be hospitable, one who loves what is good, who is self-controlled, upright, holy and disciplined.

MATTHEW IO:42
Jesus said, "If anyone gives even a cup of cold water to one of these little ones because he is my disciple, I tell you the truth, he will certainly not lose his reward."

DEUTERONOMY I5:II
Be openhanded toward your brothers and toward the poor and needy in your land.

HEBREWS I3:2
Do not forget to entertain strangers, for by so doing some people have entertained angels without knowing it.

ROMANS 12:13

Share with God's people who are in need.
Practice hospitality.

MATTHEW 25:34—40

Jesus said, "The King will say to those on his
right, 'Come, you who are blessed by my Father;
take your inheritance, the kingdom prepared for
you since the creation of the world. For I was
hungry and you gave me something to eat, I was
thirsty and you gave me something to drink, I was
a stranger and you invited me in, I needed
clothes and you clothed me, I was sick and you
looked after me, I was in prison and you came to
visit me.' Then the righteous will answer him
'Lord, when did we see you hungry and feed you,
or thirsty and give you something to drink? When
did we see you a stranger and invite you in, or
needing clothes and clothe you? When did we see
you sick or in prison and go visit you?' The King
will reply, 'I tell you the truth, whatever you did
for one of the least of these brothers of mine,
you did for me.'"

Humility

ROMANS 12:3

By the grace given me I say to every one of you:
Do not think of yourself more highly than you
ought, but rather think of yourself with sober
judgment, in accordance with the measure of
faith God has given you.

PSALM 147:6

The LORD sustains the humble
   but casts the wicked to the ground.

2 CORINTHIANS 3:5

Not that we are competent in ourselves to claim
anything for ourselves, but our competence
comes from God.

PROVERBS 16:18

Pride goes before destruction,
   a haughty spirit before a fall.

PHILIPPIANS 2:5—8

Your attitude should be the same as that
of Christ Jesus:
Who, being in very nature God,
    did not consider equality with God
    something to be grasped,
but made himself nothing,
    taking the very nature of a servant,
    being made in human likeness.
And being found in appearance as a man,
    he humbled himself
        and became obedient to death—
        even death on a cross!

I PETER 5:5

Be submissive to those who are older. All of
you, clothe yourselves with humility toward
one another, because,
    "God opposes the proud
        but gives grace to the humble."

Integrity

PROVERBS 2:7—8
> [God] holds victory in store for the upright,
>> he is a shield to those whose walk
>> is blameless,
> for he guards the course of the just
>> and protects the way of his faithful ones.

I CHRONICLES 29:17
> I know, my God, that you test the heart and are
> pleased with integrity.

PSALM 84:11
> The LORD God is a sun and shield;
>> the LORD bestows favor and honor;
> no good thing does he withhold
>> from those whose walk is blameless.

PROVERBS 10:9
> The man of integrity walks securely,
>> but he who takes crooked paths will
>> be found out.

PSALM 41:12

In my integrity you uphold me
and set me in your presence forever.

ISAIAH 57:2

Those who walk uprightly
enter into peace.

PROVERBS 16:7

When a man's ways are pleasing to the LORD,
he makes even his enemies live at
peace with him.

JAMES 2:18

Someone will say, "You have faith; I have deeds."
Show me your faith without deeds, and I will show
you my faith by what I do.

PROVERBS 11:3

The integrity of the upright guides them.

PSALM 18:25

To the faithful you show yourself faithful,
to the blameless you show yourself blameless.

JESUS

ISAIAH 7:14

The Lord himself will give you a sign: The virgin will be with child and will give birth to a son, and will call him Immanuel.

JOHN 8:12

Jesus said, "I am the light of the world. Whoever follows me will never walk in darkness, but will have the light of life."

REVELATION 3:11

Jesus said, "I am coming soon. Hold on to what you have, so that no one will take your crown."

LUKE 1:32—33

The angel said to Mary, "[Jesus] will be great and will be called the Son of the Most High. The Lord God will give him the throne of his father David, and he will reign over the house of Jacob forever; his kingdom will never end."

PHILIPPIANS 3:20

Our citizenship is in heaven. And we eagerly await
a Savior from there, the Lord Jesus Christ.

ISAIAH 11:2

The Spirit of the LORD will rest on him—
the Spirit of wisdom and of understanding,
the Spirit of counsel and of power,
the Spirit of knowledge and of the fear
of the LORD.

COLOSSIANS 3:4

When Christ, who is your life, appears, then you
also will appear with him in glory.

ISAIAH 9:6

For to us a child is born,
to us a son is given,
and the government will be on his shoulders.
And he will be called Wonderful Counselor,
Mighty God,
Everlasting Father, Prince of Peace.

JUDGMENT

PROVERBS 31:8—9

Speak up for those who cannot speak
for themselves,

for the rights of all who are destitute.
Speak up and judge fairly;

defend the rights of the poor and needy.

LUKE 6:37—38

Jesus said, "Forgive, and you will be forgiven.
Give, and it will be given to you. A good measure, pressed down, shaken together and running
over, will be poured into your lap."

2 THESSALONIANS 1:5

God's judgment is right, and as a result you will
be counted worthy of the kingdom of God.

ROMANS 14:13

Let us stop passing judgment on one another.
Instead, make up your mind not to put any stum-
bling block or obstacle in your brother's way.

ZECHARIAH 7:9

This is what the Lord Almighty says: "Administer true justice; show mercy and compassion to one another."

JAMES 2:12—13

Speak and act as those who are going to be judged by the law that gives freedom, because judgment without mercy will be shown to anyone who has not been merciful. Mercy triumphs over judgment!

ROMANS 2:1

You, therefore, have no excuse, you who pass judgment on someone else, for at whatever point you judge the other, you are condemning yourself, because you who pass judgment do the same things.

DEUTERONOMY 1:17

Do not show partiality in judging; hear both small and great alike. Do not be afraid of any man, for judgment belongs to God.

JUSTIFICATION

ROMANS 5:18—19

Just as the result of one trespass was condemnation for all men, so also the result of one act of righteousness was justification that brings life for all men. For just as through the disobedience of the one man the many were made sinners, so also through the obedience of the one man the many will be made righteous.

ROMANS 5:1

Since we have been justified through faith, we have peace with God through our Lord Jesus Christ.

2 CORINTHIANS 5:21

God made him who had no sin to be sin for us, so that in him we might become the righteousness of God.

JAMES 2:24

You see that a person is justified by what he does
and not by faith alone.

I CORINTHIANS 6:11

You were washed, you were sanctified, you were
justified in the name of the Lord Jesus Christ and
by the Spirit of our God.

GALATIANS 3:24

The law was put in charge to lead us to Christ that
we might be justified by faith.

ROMANS 3:25—26

God presented [Christ Jesus] as a sacrifice of
atonement, through faith in his blood. He did this
to demonstrate his justice, because in his forbear-
ance he had left the sins committed beforehand
unpunished—he did it to demonstrate his justice
at the present time, so as to be just and the one
who justifies those who have faith in Jesus.

Kindness

2 PETER 1:5 — 7

Make every effort to add to your faith goodness; and to goodness, knowledge; and to
knowledge, self-control; and to self-control,
perseverance; and to perseverance, godliness;
and to godliness, brotherly kindness; and to
brotherly kindness, love.

PROVERBS 11:16

A kindhearted woman gains respect,
 but ruthless men gain only wealth.

EPHESIANS 4:32

Be kind and compassionate to one another,
forgiving each other, just as in Christ God
forgave you.

PROVERBS 11:17

A kind man benefits himself,
 but a cruel man brings trouble on himself.

1 PETER 3:8

All of you, live in harmony with one another; be sympathetic, love as brothers, be compassionate and humble.

PROVERBS 14:31

Whoever is kind to the needy honors God.

MATTHEW 7:12

Jesus said, "In everything, do to others what you would have them do to you, for this sums up the Law and the Prophets."

PROVERBS 19:17

He who is kind to the poor lends to the LORD,
    and he will reward him for what he has done.

1 CORINTHIANS 13:4

Love is patient, love is kind. It does not envy, it does not boast, it is not proud.

1 THESSALONIANS 5:15

Make sure that nobody pays back wrong for wrong, but always try to be kind to each other and to everyone else.

LEADERSHIP

PROVERBS 16:12

Kings detest wrongdoing,
for a throne is established
through righteousness.

LUKE 22:26

Jesus said, "The greatest among you should be
like the youngest, and the one who rules like the
one who serves."

PROVERBS 20:28

Love and faithfulness keep a king safe;
through love his throne is made secure.

ROMANS 12:6 — 8

We have different gifts, according to the grace
given us...If a man's gift is serving, let him serve;
if it is teaching, let him teach; if it is encouraging,
let him encourage; if it is contributing to the
needs of others, let him give generously; if it is
leadership, let him govern diligently; if it is
showing mercy, let him do it cheerfully.

PSALM 2:10 — 11

Therefore, you kings, be wise;
   be warned, you rulers of the earth.
Serve the LORD with fear
   and rejoice with trembling.

2 CHRONICLES 1:10 — 12

Solomon said, "Give me wisdom and knowledge,
that I may lead this people, for who is able to govern this great people of yours?" God said to
Solomon, "Since this is your heart's desire and you
have not asked for wealth, riches or honor, nor
for the death of your enemies, and since you have
not asked for a long life but for wisdom and
knowledge to govern my people over whom I have
made you king, therefore wisdom and knowledge
will be given you. And I will also give you wealth,
riches and honor, such as no king who was before
you ever had and none after you will have."

JOSHUA 1:6

The LORD said to Joshua, "Be strong and
courageous, because you will lead these people
to inherit the land I swore to their forefathers
to give them."

LIFE

ROMANS 8:2

Through Christ Jesus the law of the Spirit of life set me free from the law of sin and death.

JOHN 6:35

Jesus declared, "I am the bread of life. He who comes to me will never go hungry, and he who believes in me will never be thirsty."

COLOSSIANS 3:1 — 4

Set your hearts on things above, where Christ is seated at the right hand of God. Set your minds on things above, not on earthly things. For you died, and your life is now hidden with Christ in God. When Christ, who is your life, appears, then you also will appear with him in glory.

ROMANS 6:11

Count yourselves dead to sin but alive to God in Christ Jesus.

PSALM 16:11

You have made known to me the path of life;
    you will fill me with joy in your presence, with
    eternal pleasures at your right hand.

JOHN 6:63

Jesus said, "The Spirit gives life; the flesh counts
for nothing. The words I have spoken to you are
spirit and they are life."

ROMANS 8:11

If the Spirit of him who raised Jesus from the dead
is living in you, he who raised Christ from the
dead will also give life to your mortal bodies
through his Spirit, who lives in you.

JOB 33:4

The Spirit of God has made me;
    the breath of the Almighty gives me life.

PROVERBS 3:1 — 2

My son, do not forget my teaching,
    but keep my commands in your heart,
for they will prolong your life many years
    and bring you prosperity.

LOVE

1 JOHN 4:16

God is love. Whoever lives in love lives in God,
and God in him.

1 JOHN 4:7

Dear friends, let us love one another, for love
comes from God. Everyone who loves has been
born of God and knows God.

COLOSSIANS 3:12 — 14

As God's chosen people, holy and dearly loved,
clothe yourselves with compassion, kindness,
humility, gentleness and patience. Bear with each
other and forgive whatever grievances you may
have against one another. Forgive as the Lord
forgave you. And over all these virtues put on love,
which binds them all together in perfect unity.

1 THESSALONIANS 4:9

You yourselves have been taught by God to love
each other.

I CORINTHIANS 13:13 — 14:1

These three remain: faith, hope and love. But the greatest of these is love. Follow the way of love.

I THESSALONIANS 3:12

May the Lord make your love increase and overflow for each other and for everyone else.

I TIMOTHY 1:5

The goal of this command is love, which comes from a pure heart and a good conscience and a sincere faith.

ROMANS 12:9 — 10

Love must be sincere. Hate what is evil; cling to what is good. Be devoted to one another in brotherly love. Honor one another above yourselves.

LOVING GOD

PSALM 31:23

Love the LORD, all his saints!
    The LORD preserves the faithful,
but the proud he pays back in full.

PSALM 37:4

Delight yourself in the LORD
    and he will give you the desires of your heart.

DEUTERONOMY 7:9

Know therefore that the LORD your God is God;
he is the faithful God, keeping his covenant of
love to a thousand generations of those who love
him and keep his commands.

PSALM 73:25—26

Whom have I in heaven but you?
    And earth has nothing I desire besides you.
My flesh and my heart may fail,
    but God is the strength of my heart
    and my portion forever.

MATTHEW 22:37 — 38

Jesus replied: "'Love the Lord your God with all your heart and with all your soul and with all your mind.' This is the first and greatest commandment."

PSALM 91:14

"Because he loves me," says the LORD, "I will rescue him;
I will protect him, for he acknowledges my name."

PSALM 145:20

The LORD watches over all who love him,
but all the wicked he will destroy.

ROMANS 8:28

We know that in all things God works for the good of those who love him, who have been called according to his purpose.

I CORINTHIANS 8:3

The man who loves God is known by God.

Materialism

MATTHEW 19:21

Jesus answered, "If you want to be perfect, go, sell your possessions and give to the poor, and you will have treasure in heaven. Then come, follow me."

PROVERBS 3:9 — 10

Honor the LORD with your wealth,
   with the firstfruits of all your crops;
then your barns will be filled to overflowing,
   and your vats will brim over with new wine.

1 TIMOTHY 6:6 — 8

Godliness with contentment is great gain. For we brought nothing into the world, and we can take nothing out of it. But if we have food and clothing, we will be content with that.

PROVERBS 13:22

A good man leaves an inheritance for his
children's children,
> but a sinner's wealth is stored up for
> the righteous.

MATTHEW 6:31, 33

Jesus said, "Do not worry, saying, 'What shall we
eat?' or 'What shall we drink?' or 'What shall we
wear?' ... But seek first his kingdom and his righteousness, and all these things will be given to you
as well."

PROVERBS 19:17

He who is kind to the poor lends to the LORD,
> and he will reward him for what he has done.

ECCLESIASTES 5:19

When God gives any man wealth and possessions,
and enables him to enjoy them, to accept his lot
and be happy in his work—this is a gift of God.

PROVERBS 11:25

A generous man will prosper;
> he who refreshes others will himself
> be refreshed.

what really matters

American is the "Land of Cool!" You see it all around you. Do this, wear that, buy this, carry that, say this—and you'll be cool. Trouble is, the rules of coolness have been known to change overnight. You just get your hands on the right CD or find a pair of pants with the right logo, and bam! Something new pops up. How's a girl supposed to cope?

For one thing, you should understand that "real" coolness has nothing to do with what you have or what you wear. It comes from within. What kind of person are you on the inside? God—the coolest of the cool—wants you to know that who you are is much more important than what you wear or what you own.

God is so "not" impressed with your hip movie collection or your trendy clothing. What impresses him are your inner riches, things like courage and loyalty, truthfulness and kindness, thankfulness and compassion. Which standard of coolness are you going to pursue? The ever-changing, worldly kind or the never-changing, godly kind?

You can spend your time running after each new fad, trying to find ways to look good to others, sacrificing your own personal style in order to fit in. But wouldn't it be better to please God, to become the unique person he created you to be?

Make up your mind to value the things that really matter. That doesn't mean you can't enjoy the good things that come your way. It doesn't mean you can't wear fashionable clothes or listen to popular music. It just means that you choose those things based on who you are rather than who other people want or expect you to be. What good would it be if others thought you were the coolest girl around, if you weren't cool to yourself? Don't be a material girl; keep your eyes on the things that really matter.

Maturity

I PETER 2:2

Like newborn babies, crave pure spiritual milk,
so that by it you may grow up in your salvation.

EPHESIANS 4:11—13

It was [Christ] who gave some to be apostles,
some to be prophets, some to be evangelists, and
some to be pastors and teachers, to prepare
God's people for works of service, so that the
body of Christ may be built up until we all reach
unity in the faith and in the knowledge of the
Son of God and become mature, attaining to the
whole measure of the fullness of Christ.

PSALM 90:12

Teach us to number our days aright,
    that we may gain a heart of wisdom.

HEBREWS 6:1

Let us leave the elementary teachings about
Christ and go on to maturity.

PROVERBS 9:9

Instruct a wise man and he will be wiser still;
teach a righteous man and he will add to
his learning.

PHILIPPIANS 1:6

[God] who began a good work in you will carry it
on to completion until the day of Christ Jesus.

HEBREWS 5:13—14

Anyone who lives on milk, being still an infant, is
not acquainted with the teaching about righteousness. But solid food is for the mature, who by constant use have trained themselves to distinguish
good from evil.

EPHESIANS 4:15

Instead, speaking the truth in love, we will in
all things grow up into him who is the Head, that
is, Christ.

JAMES 1:4

Perseverance must finish its work so that you may
be mature and complete, not lacking anything.

Money

PROVERBS 13:11

He who gathers money little by little makes it grow.

PHILIPPIANS 4:19

My God will meet all your needs according to his glorious riches in Christ Jesus.

PROVERBS 13:22

A good man leaves an inheritance for his children's children,
>but a sinner's wealth is stored up for the righteous.

LUKE 12:15

Jesus said to them, "Watch out! Be on your guard against all kinds of greed; a man's life does not consist in the abundance of his possessions."

HEBREWS 13:5

Keep your lives free from the love of money
and be content with what you have, because
God has said,
"Never will I leave you;
never will I forsake you."

PROVERBS 3:9 — 10

Honor the LORD with your wealth,
with the firstfruits of all your crops;
then your barns will be filled to overflowing,
and your vats will brim over with new wine.

LUKE 16:10

Jesus said, "Whoever can be trusted with very
little can also be trusted with much, and
whoever is dishonest with very little will also
be dishonest with much."

MATTHEW 6:31 — 33

Jesus said, "Do not worry, saying, 'What shall
we eat?' or 'What shall we drink?' or 'What shall
we wear?' For the pagans run after all these
things, and your heavenly Father knows that
you need them."

OBEDIENCE

MATTHEW 7:24—25

Jesus said, "Everyone who hears these words of mine and puts them into practice is like a wise man who built his house on the rock. The rain came down, the streams rose, and the winds blew and beat against that house; yet it did not fall, because it had its foundation on the rock."

ROMANS 2:13

It is not those who hear the law who are righteous in God's sight, but it is those who obey the law who will be declared righteous.

LUKE 11:28

Jesus replied, "Blessed rather are those who hear the word of God and obey it."

MATTHEW 5:19

Jesus said, "Whoever practices and teaches these commands will be called great in the kingdom of heaven."

DEUTERONOMY 13:4

It is the LORD your God you must follow, and him you must revere. Keep his commands and obey him; serve him and hold fast to him.

I JOHN 2:5

If anyone obeys his word, God's love is truly made complete in him. This is how we know we are in him: Whoever claims to live in him must walk as Jesus did.

JOHN 15:10 — 11

Jesus said, "If you obey my commands, you will remain in my love, just as I have obeyed my Father's commands and remain in his love. I have told you this so that my joy may be in you and that your joy may be complete."

JOB 36:11

If they obey and serve him,
    they will spend the rest of their days
        in prosperity
    and their years in contentment.

Patience

PROVERBS 19:11

A man's wisdom gives him patience;
it is to his glory to overlook an offense.

PSALM 40:1

I waited patiently for the LORD;
he turned to me and heard my cry.

JAMES 5:7—8

Be patient ... until the Lord's coming. See how
the farmer waits for the land to yield its valuable
crop and how patient he is for the autumn and
spring rains. You too, be patient and stand firm,
because the Lord's coming is near.

COLOSSIANS 3:13

Bear with each other and forgive whatever grievances you may have against one another. Forgive
as the Lord forgave you.

1 THESSALONIANS 5:14

Warn those who are idle, encourage the timid, help the weak, be patient with everyone.

PROVERBS 14:29

A patient man has great understanding,
    but a quick-tempered man displays folly.

ROMANS 12:12

Be joyful in hope, patient in affliction, faithful in prayer.

EPHESIANS 4:2

Be completely humble and gentle; be patient, bearing with one another in love.

PROVERBS 12:16

A fool shows his annoyance at once,
    but a prudent man overlooks an insult.

ECCLESIASTES 7:8

The end of a matter is better than its beginning,
    and patience is better than pride.

GALATIANS 6:9

Let us not become weary in doing good, for at the proper time we will reap a harvest if we do not give up.

PERSEVERANCE

2 CORINTHIANS 4:17
Our light and momentary troubles are achieving for us an eternal glory that far outweighs them all.

ROMANS 2:7
To those who by persistence in doing good seek glory, honor and immortality, he will give eternal life.

JAMES 1:12
Blessed is the man who perseveres under trial, because when he has stood the test, he will receive the crown of life that God has promised to those who love him.

1 PETER 5:10
The God of all grace, who called you to his eternal glory in Christ, after you have suffered a little while, will himself restore you and make you strong, firm and steadfast.

JAMES 1:4

Perseverance must finish its work so that you may
be mature and complete, not lacking anything.

PSALM 119:50

My comfort in my suffering is this:
    Your promise preserves my life.

PSALM 17:5

My steps have held to your paths;
    my feet have not slipped.

GALATIANS 6:9

Let us not become weary in doing good, for at the
proper time we will reap a harvest if we do not
give up.

PSALM 126:5

Those who sow in tears
    will reap with songs of joy.

PROVERBS 14:23

All hard work brings a profit,
    but mere talk leads only to poverty.

PRAYER

2 CHRONICLES 7:14

"If my people, who are called by my name, will humble themselves and pray and seek my face and turn from their wicked ways, then will I hear from heaven and will forgive their sin and will heal their land," says the LORD.

DEUTERONOMY 4:7

What other nation is so great as to have their gods near them the way the LORD our God is near us whenever we pray to him?

MATTHEW 26:41

Jesus said, "Watch and pray so that you will not fall into temptation. The spirit is willing, but the body is weak."

JEREMIAH 29:12

"You will call upon me and come and pray to me, and I will listen to you," declares the LORD.

MARK 11:25

Jesus said, "When you stand praying, if you hold anything against anyone, forgive him, so that your Father in heaven may forgive you your sins."

COLOSSIANS 4:2

Devote yourselves to prayer, being watchful and thankful.

I THESSALONIANS 5:17

Pray continually.

JAMES 5:15

The prayer offered in faith will make the sick person well; the Lord will raise him up. If he has sinned, he will be forgiven.

EPHESIANS 6:18

Pray in the Spirit on all occasions with all kinds of prayers and requests. With this in mind, be alert and always keep on praying for all the saints.

the practice of prayer

How often should you pray? A likely answer might be, "Once in the morning and once at night," or, "Definitely before every meal." Some people only pray when they're in a bind and need God's help. You might be surprised to know what the Bible says about how much Christians should pray. It says we should pray all the time, in fact, "continually" (1 Thessalonians 5:17).

That can't be right—when's a girl supposed to sleep, study, catch up with friends? Not to worry—you don't need to start packing for the convent just yet. Sometimes when the Bible talks about something that's very important, it states it in extreme terms in order to make an impact. It's like a teacher saying, "Study your brains out!" The teacher wants to make it abundantly clear to her students that they should study hard. What the Bible is making clear is that Christians should pray a lot. But what is prayer, really?

136

It's important to understand that prayer isn't like slipping money into a big vending machine, pushing the right selection, and getting the answer you want. God does hear and answer your prayers, in his time and in his way. That may mean "no," just like when your parents say no to those things that are not in your best interest.

It's the same with God, except in one important way: Parents are human, and they make mistakes, but God never does. His greatest concern is that you become the best woman you can be on the inside.

There isn't anything you can't talk to God about—nothing will surprise him. Practice praying throughout your day, even if you're just saying, "God, I know you're here with me. Thanks."

Try to take some time during your week, as Jesus did when he was here on earth, to spend praying alone, in quiet. The more you talk to God, the easier it will be. And when prayer is part of everything you do and say, then you are, in a sense, praying continually!

PRIORITIES

2 CORINTHIANS 5:9

We make it our goal to please [the Lord],
whether we are at home in the body or away
from it.

MATTHEW 6:24

Jesus said, "No one can serve two masters. Either
he will hate the one and love the other, or he
will be devoted to the one and despise the other.
You cannot serve both God and Money."

ECCLESIASTES 12:13

Now all has been heard;
    here is the conclusion of the matter:
Fear God and keep his commandments,
    for this is the whole duty of man.

MATTHEW 6:33

Jesus said, "Seek first his kingdom and his righteousness, and all these things will be given to
you as well."

I PETER 2:2-3

Like newborn babies, crave pure spiritual milk, so that by it you may grow up in your salvation, now that you have tasted that the Lord is good.

PHILIPPIANS 3:13—14

Forgetting what is behind and straining toward what is ahead, I press on toward the goal to win the prize for which God has called me heavenward in Christ Jesus.

PROVERBS 21:21

He who pursues righteousness and love
   finds life, prosperity and honor.

2 TIMOTHY 2:22

Flee the evil desires of youth, and pursue righteousness, faith, love and peace, along with those who call on the Lord out of a pure heart.

I KINGS 22:5

Jehoshaphat also said to the king of Israel, "First seek the counsel of the LORD."

REDEMPTION

ISAIAH 44:22

"I have swept away your offenses like a cloud,
your sins like the morning mist.
Return to me,
for I have redeemed you," declares the LORD.

LAMENTATIONS 3:57—58

You came near when I called you,
and you said, "Do not fear."
O LORD, you took up my case;
you redeemed my life.

I CORINTHIANS 1:30

It is because of him that you are in Christ Jesus,
who has become for us wisdom from God—that
is, our righteousness, holiness and redemption.

EPHESIANS 1:7

In [Christ] we have redemption through his blood,
the forgiveness of sins, in accordance with the
riches of God's grace.

HEBREWS 9:12

[Christ] did not enter by means of the blood of goats and calves; but he entered the Most Holy Place once for all by his own blood, having obtained eternal redemption.

GALATIANS 3:13

Christ redeemed us from the curse of the law by becoming a curse for us.

COLOSSIANS 1:13 — 14

[God] has rescued us from the dominion of darkness and brought us into the kingdom of the Son he loves, in whom we have redemption, the forgiveness of sins.

JOB 33:28

He redeemed my soul from going down to the pit,
    and I will live to enjoy the light.'

EXODUS 15:13

"In your unfailing love you will lead
    the people you have redeemed.
In your strength you will guide them
    to your holy dwelling.

Relationships

ECCLESIASTES 4:9—10

Two are better than one,
    because they have a good return
    for their work:
If one falls down,
    his friend can help him up.
But pity the man who falls
    and has no one to help him up!

EPHESIANS 4:32

Be kind and compassionate to one another,
forgiving each other, just as in Christ God
forgave you.

REVELATION 3:20

Jesus said, "Here I am! I stand at the door and
knock. If anyone hears my voice and opens the
door, I will come in and eat with him, and he
with me."

MATTHEW 25:40

Jesus said, "I tell you the truth, whatever you did for one of the least of these brothers of mine, you did for me."

MATTHEW 5:43—45

Jesus said, "You have heard that it was said, 'Love your neighbor and hate your enemy.' But I tell you: Love your enemies and pray for those who persecute you, that you may be sons of your Father in heaven."

PROVERBS 13:20

He who walks with the wise grows wise.

MATTHEW 22:39

Jesus replied, "'Love your neighbor as yourself.'"

JOHN 13:35

Jesus said, "By this all men will know that you are my disciples, if you love one another."

GALATIANS 6:2

Carry each other's burdens, and in this way you will fulfill the law of Christ.

GALATIANS 6:10

Therefore, as we have opportunity, let us do good to all people, especially to those who belong to the family of believers.

REPEПTAПCE

EZEKIEL 18:21

"If a wicked man turns away from all the sins he has committed and keeps all my decrees and does what is just and right, he will surely live; he will not die," says the LORD

ACTS 2:38

Peter replied, "Repent and be baptized, every one of you, in the name of Jesus Christ for the forgiveness of your sins. And you will receive the gift of the Holy Spirit."

2 PETER 3:9

The Lord is not slow in keeping his promise, as some understand slowness. He is patient with you, not wanting anyone to perish, but everyone to come to repentance.

LUKE 17:3—4

Jesus said, "If your brother sins, rebuke him, and if he repents, forgive him. If he sins against you seven times in a day, and seven times comes back to you and says, 'I repent,' forgive him."

ACTS 3:19

Repent, then, and turn to God, so that your sins may be wiped out, that times of refreshing may come from the Lord, and that he may send the Christ, who has been appointed for you—even Jesus.

LUKE 15:7

Jesus said, "There will be more rejoicing in heaven over one sinner who repents than over ninety-nine righteous persons who do not need to repent."

I JOHN 1:9

If we confess our sins, he is faithful and just and will forgive us our sins and purify us from all unrighteousness.

ISAIAH 30:15

This is what the Sovereign LORD, the Holy One of Israel, says:
"In repentance and rest is your salvation,
    in quietness and trust is your strength..."

Repu†a†ion

ISAIAH 62:2

The nations will see your righteousness,
and all kings your glory;
you will be called by a new name
that the mouth of the LORD will bestow.

LUKE 14:12 — 14

Jesus said to his host, "When you give a lunch-
eon or dinner, do not invite your friends, your
brothers or relatives, or your rich neighbors; if
you do, they may invite you back and so you
will be repaid. But when you give a banquet,
invite the poor, the crippled, the lame, the
blind, and you will be blessed. Although they
cannot repay you, you will be repaid at the
resurrection of the righteous."

MATTHEW 23:11 — 12

Jesus said, "The greatest among you will be
your servant. For whoever exalts himself will
be humbled, and whoever humbles himself will
be exalted."

TITUS 1:7—8

Since an overseer is entrusted with God's work, he must be blameless—not overbearing, not quick-tempered, not given to drunkenness, not violent, not pursuing dishonest gain. Rather he must be hospitable, one who loves what is good, who is self-controlled, upright, holy and disciplined.

PROVERBS 22:1

A good name is more desirable than great riches;
   to be esteemed is better than silver or gold.

HEBREWS 11:24—26

By faith Moses, when he had grown up, refused to be known as the son of Pharaoh's daughter. He chose to be mistreated along with the people of God rather than to enjoy the pleasures of sin for a short time. He regarded disgrace for the sake of Christ as of greater value than the treasures of Egypt, because he was looking ahead to his reward.

LUKE 14:10

But when you are invited, take the lowest place, so that when your host comes, he will say to you, 'Friend, move up to a better place.' Then you will be honored in the presence of all your fellow guests.

RESPONSIBILITY

MATTHEW 25:20—21

The man who had received the five talents brought the other five. "Master," he said, "you entrusted me with five talents. See, I have gained five more."

His master replied, "Well done, good and faithful servant! You have been faithful with a few things; I will put you in charge of many things. Come and share your master's happiness!"

2 TIMOTHY 2:2

The things you have heard me say in the presence of many witnesses entrust to reliable men who will also be qualified to teach others.

1 CORINTHIANS 3:8

The man who plants and the man who waters have one purpose, and each will be rewarded according to his own labor.

MATTHEW 5:14-16

Jesus said, "You are the light of the world. A city on a hill cannot be hidden. Neither do people light a lamp and put it under a bowl. Instead they put it on its stand, and it gives light to everyone in the house. In the same way, let your light shine before men, that they may see your good deeds and praise your Father in heaven."

EZEKIEL 18:5, 9

"Suppose there is a righteous man
    who does what is just and right...
He follows my decrees
    and faithfully keeps my laws.
That man is righteous;
    he will surely live,"
declares the Sovereign LORD.

1 PETER 2:9

But you are a chosen people, a royal priesthood, a holy nation, a people belonging to God, that you may declare the praises of him who called you out of darkness into his wonderful light.

1 CORINTHIANS 4:2

Now it is required that those who have been given a trust must prove faithful.

Righteousness

ISAIAH 32:17

The fruit of righteousness will be peace;
the effect of righteousness will be quietness
and confidence forever.

MATTHEW 5:6

Jesus said,
"Blessed are those who hunger and thirst for
righteousness,
for they will be filled."

PROVERBS 12:28

In the way of righteousness there is life;
along that path is immortality.

PSALM 112:6—7

Surely he will never be shaken;
a righteous man will be remembered forever.
He will have no fear of bad news;
his heart is steadfast, trusting in the LORD.

HOSEA 10:12

Sow for yourselves righteousness,
    reap the fruit of unfailing love,
and break up your unplowed ground;
    for it is time to seek the LORD,
until he comes
    and showers righteousness on you.

PSALM 37:30–31

The mouth of the righteous man utters wisdom,
    and his tongue speaks what is just.
The law of his God is in his heart;
    his feet do not slip.

JAMES 1:27

Religion that God our Father accepts as pure and
faultless is this: to look after orphans and widows
in their distress and to keep oneself from being
polluted by the world.

PROVERBS 21:21

He who pursues righteousness and love
    finds life, prosperity and honor.

JOB 36:7

[God] does not take his eyes off the righteous;
    he enthrones them with kings
    and exalts them forever.

1 PETER 3:12

The eyes of the Lord are on the righteous
    and his ears are attentive to their prayer.

Salvation

1 TIMOTHY 2:3—4

God our Savior ... wants all men to be saved and to come to a knowledge of the truth.

ROMANS 10:9

If you confess with your mouth, "Jesus is Lord," and believe in your heart that God raised him from the dead, you will be saved.

HEBREWS 5:9

Once made perfect, [Christ] became the source of eternal salvation for all who obey him.

2 CORINTHIANS 6:2

[God] says,
"In the time of my favor I heard you,
and in the day of salvation I helped you."
I tell you, now is the time of God's favor, now is the day of salvation.

TITUS 3:4 — 5

When the kindness and love of God our Savior appeared, he saved us, not because of righteous things we had done, but because of his mercy. He saved us through the washing of rebirth and renewal by the Holy Spirit.

ACTS 10:43

All the prophets testify about [Jesus] that everyone who believes in him receives forgiveness of sins through his name.

MARK 16:16

Jesus said, "Whoever believes and is baptized will be saved, but whoever does not believe will be condemned."

I THESSALONIANS 5:9 — 10

God did not appoint us to suffer wrath but to receive salvation through our Lord Jesus Christ. He died for us so that, whether we are awake or asleep, we may live together with him.

Self-Control

I THESSALONIANS 5:8

Since we belong to the day, let us be self-controlled, putting on faith and love as a breastplate, and the hope of salvation as a helmet.

I PETER 4:7

The end of all things is near. Therefore be clear minded and self-controlled so that you can pray.

HEBREWS 2:18

Because he himself suffered when he was tempted, Christ is able to help those who are being tempted.

TITUS 2:11 — 13

The grace of God that brings salvation has appeared to all men. It teaches us to say "No" to ungodliness and worldly passions, and to live self-controlled, upright and godly lives in this present age, while we wait for the blessed hope— the glorious appearing of our great God and Savior, Jesus Christ.

I PETER 1:13

Prepare your minds for action; be self-controlled; set your hope fully on the grace to be given you when Jesus Christ is revealed.

ROMANS 8:13

If you live according to the sinful nature, you will die; but if by the Spirit you put to death the misdeeds of the body, you will live.

MATTHEW 16:24

Jesus said to his disciples, "If anyone would come after me, he must deny himself and take up his cross and follow me."

I PETER 5:8

Be self-controlled and alert. Your enemy the devil prowls around like a roaring lion looking for someone to devour.

SERVICE

I CHRONICLES 28:9

Acknowledge the God of your father, and serve him with wholehearted devotion and with a willing mind, for the LORD searches every heart and understands every motive behind the thoughts.

EPHESIANS 6:7—8

Serve wholeheartedly, as if you were serving the Lord, not men, because you know that the Lord will reward everyone for whatever good he does.

I PETER 4:10—11

Each one should use whatever gift he has received to serve others, faithfully administering God's grace in its various forms. If anyone speaks, he should do it as one speaking the very words of God. If anyone serves, he should do it with the strength God provides, so that in all things God may be praised through Jesus Christ.

EPHESIANS 4:11 — 13

It was [Christ] who gave some to be apostles, some to be prophets, some to be evangelists, and some to be pastors and teachers, to prepare God's people for works of service, so that the body of Christ may be built up until we all reach unity in the faith and in the knowledge of the Son of God and become mature, attaining to the whole measure of the fullness of Christ.

COLOSSIANS 3:23 — 24

Whatever you do, work at it with all your heart, as working for the Lord, not for men, since you know that you will receive an inheritance from the Lord as a reward. It is the Lord Christ you are serving.

MATTHEW 20:25-26

Jesus called them together and said, "You know that the rulers of the Gentiles lord it over them, and their high officials exercise authority over them. Not so with you. Instead, whoever wants to become great among you must be your servant."

DEUTERONOMY 10:12 — 13

And now, O Israel, what does the LORD your God ask of you but to fear the LORD your God, to walk in all his ways, to love him, to serve the LORD your God with all your heart and with all your soul, and to observe the LORD's commands and decrees that I am giving you today for your own good?

Sin

I JOHN 2:2

[Jesus] is the atoning sacrifice for our sins, and not only for ours but also for the sins of the whole world.

ROMANS 6:12, 14

Do not let sin reign in your mortal body so that you obey its evil desires....For sin shall not be your master, because you are not under law, but under grace.

I JOHN 1:9

If we confess our sins, he is faithful and just and will forgive us our sins and purify us from all unrighteousness.

ROMANS 5:19

Just as through the disobedience of the one man the many were made sinners, so also through the obedience of the one man the many will be made righteous.

LUKE 15:10

Jesus said, "I tell you, there is rejoicing in the presence of the angels of God over one sinner who repents."

ISAIAH 55:7

Let the wicked forsake his way
    and the evil man his thoughts.
Let him turn to the LORD, and he will have
mercy on him,
        and to our God, for he will freely pardon.

2 CHRONICLES 7:14

"If my people, who are called by my name, will humble themselves and pray and seek my face and turn from their wicked ways, then will I hear from heaven and will forgive their sin and will heal their land," declares the LORD.

PSALM 32:5

Then I acknowledged my sin to you
    and did not cover up my iniquity.
I said, "I will confess
    my transgressions to the LORD"
and you forgave
    the guilt of my sin.

STEWARDSHIP

COLOSSIANS 3:23 — 24

Whatever you do, work at it with all your heart, as working for the Lord, not for men, since you know that you will receive an inheritance from the Lord as a reward. It is the Lord Christ you are serving.

LUKE 12:42 — 43

The Lord answered, "Who then is the faithful and wise manager, whom the master puts in charge of his servants to give them their food allowance at the proper time? It will be good for that servant whom the master finds doing so when he returns."

PSALM 112:5

Good will come to him who is generous and lends freely,
   who conduct his affairs with justice.

I CORINTHIANS 4:2

It is required that those who have been given a trust must prove faithful.

MALACHI 3:10

"Bring the whole tithe into the storehouse, that there may be food in my house. Test me in this," says the LORD Almighty, "and see if I will not throw open the floodgates of heaven and pour out so much blessing that you will not have room enough for it."

I PETER 4:10 — 11

Each one should use whatever gift he has received to serve others, faithfully administering God's grace in its various forms. If anyone speaks, he should do it as one speaking the very words of God. If anyone serves, he should do it with the strength God provides, so that in all things God may be praised through Jesus Christ.

LUKE 16:10

Whoever can be trusted with very little can also be trusted with much, and whoever is dishonest with very little will also be dishonest with much.

Talents and Gifts

ROMANS 12:6 — 8

We have different gifts, according to the grace given us. If a man's gift is prophesying, let him use it in proportion to his faith. If it is serving, let him serve; if it is teaching, let him teach; if it is encouraging, let him encourage; if it is contributing to the needs of others, let him give generously; if it is leadership, let him govern diligently; if it is showing mercy, let him do it cheerfully.

JAMES 1:17

Every good and perfect gift is from above, coming down from the Father of the heavenly lights, who does not change like shifting shadows.

I CORINTHIANS 12:4 — 7

There are different kinds of gifts, but the same Spirit. There are different kinds of service, but the same Lord. There are different kinds of working, but the same God works all of them in all men. Now to each one the manifestation of the Spirit is given for the common good.

I PETER 4:10
Each one should use whatever gift he has received
to serve others, faithfully administering God's
grace in its various forms.

ROMANS 11:29
God's gifts and his call are irrevocable.

I CORINTHIANS 7:7
Each man has his own gift from God; one has this
gift, another has that.

JOHN 3:21
But whoever lives by the truth comes into the
light, so that it may be seen plainly that what he
has done has been done through God."

PSALM 61:5
For you have heard my vows, O God;
   you have given me the heritage of those who
fear your name.

Temptation

HEBREWS 2:18

Because [Jesus] himself suffered when he was tempted, he is able to help those who are being tempted.

EPHESIANS 6:10 — 11

Be strong in the Lord and in his mighty power. Put on the full armor of God so that you can take your stand against the devil's schemes.

1 CORINTHIANS 10:13

No temptation has seized you except what is common to man. And God is faithful; he will not let you be tempted beyond what you can bear. But when you are tempted, he will also provide a way out so that you can stand up under it.

JAMES 4:7

Submit yourselves, then, to God. Resist the devil, and he will flee from you.

GALATIANS 5:1

It is for freedom that Christ has set us free.
Stand firm, then, and do not let yourselves be
burdened again by a yoke of slavery.

HEBREWS 4:14—16

Since we have a great high priest who has gone
through the heavens, Jesus the Son of God, let us
hold firmly to the faith we profess. For we do
not have a high priest who is unable to sympa-
thize with our weaknesses, but we have one who
has been tempted in every way, just as we are—
yet was without sin. Let us then approach the
throne of grace with confidence, so that we may
receive mercy and find grace to help us in our
time of need.

MATTHEW 26:41

Jesus said, "Watch and pray so that you will not
fall into temptation. The spirit is willing, but the
body is weak."

ROMANS 7:5—6

For when we were controlled by the sinful
nature, the sinful passions aroused by the law
were at work in our bodies, so that we bore
fruit for death. But now, by dying to what once
bound us, we have been released from the law
so that we serve in the new way of the Spirit,
and not in the old way of the written code.

THANKFULNESS

COLOSSIANS 2:6 — 7

Just as you received Christ Jesus as Lord,
continue to live in him, rooted and built up in
him, strengthened in the faith as you were taught,
and overflowing with thankfulness.

I CHRONICLES 16:34

Give thanks to the LORD, for he is good;
    his love endures forever.

PSALM 107:8 — 9

Let them give thanks to the LORD for his
unfailing love
    and his wonderful deeds for men,
for he satisfies the thirsty
    and fills the hungry with good things.

COLOSSIANS 3:16

Let the word of Christ dwell in you richly as you
teach and admonish one another with all wisdom,
and as you sing psalms, hymns and spiritual songs
with gratitude in your hearts to God.

PSALM 30:11—12
> You turned my wailing into dancing;
>> you removed my sackcloth and clothed
>> me with joy,
> that my heart may sing to you and not be silent.
>> O LORD my God, I will give you
>> thanks forever.

HEBREWS 12:28
> Since we are receiving a kingdom that cannot be
> shaken, let us be thankful, and so worship God
> acceptably with reverence and awe.

I THESSALONIANS 5:18
> Give thanks in all circumstances, for this is God's
> will for you in Christ Jesus.

PSALM 28:7
> The LORD is my strength and my shield;
>> my heart trusts in him, and I am helped.
> My heart leaps for joy
>> and I will give thanks to him in song.

Thankful from the
inside-out

Your confirmation class instructor probably spoke about the importance of being thankful—something your parents have most likely worked to impress on you as well. Do you realize that you have something to be thankful for the moment you wake in the morning? You woke up! You're in a warm, comfy bed under a solid roof. You probably have clothes to wear and several boxes of cereal in the pantry. And while you might not consider it a blessing right now, you're getting a good education. These are just the first hours of your day—imagine all the possibilities that lie ahead!

The Bible says over and over to give thanks, to express gratitude to God by praying, singing, and telling others what God has done in your life. One reason for this is pretty obvious: God deserves thanks. After all, he fashioned you and gave you life.

When you are focusing on what you're thankful for, it's hard to be unhappy. Thankfulness is the enemy of discontent, of always wanting something different, better, or more. You know how it feels when you're not satisfied with the way things are in your life. (Everyone does!) You wish that you had your own bedroom, or that you had a better wardrobe, or that your parents had a bigger house with a pool. When you spend time wanting what you don't have, you become more and more dissatisfied until you can't be joyful about anything. That's no way to live, and that is not the way God wants you to spend your precious energy.

The Bible says to "give thanks in all circumstances" (1 Thessalonians 5:18). You might be wondering how this is possible, especially when nothing seems to be going your way.

Having a thankful heart doesn't happen overnight. As with learning an instrument, you practice, practice, practice, and at some point, the notes flow into beautiful music. When you make the effort to be thankful as you go about your day, you'll be surprised at how much easier it will become to feel gratitude, even in the midst of hard times. What comes from your grateful heart will be glorious music to God's ears.

✝ TRUTH

PROVERBS 16:13

Kings take pleasure in honest lips;
  they value a man who speaks the truth.

JOHN 8:32

Jesus said, "You will know the truth, and the
truth will set you free."

PSALM 145:18

The LORD is near to all who call on him,
  to all who call on him in truth.

JOHN 14:6

Jesus answered, "I am the way and the truth and
the life. No one comes to the Father except
through me."

JOHN 16:13

Jesus said, "When he, the Spirit of truth, comes,
he will guide you into all truth. He will not speak
on his own; he will speak only what he hears,
and he will tell you what is yet to come."

PSALM 119:160

All your words are true;
    all your righteous laws are eternal.

1 JOHN 5:20

We know also that the Son of God has come and
has given us understanding, so that we may know
him who is true. And we are in him who is true—
even in his Son Jesus Christ. He is the true God
and eternal life.

PROVERBS 23:23

Buy the truth and do not sell it;
    get wisdom, discipline and understanding.

PSALM 86:11

Teach me your way, O LORD,
    and I will walk in your truth;
give me an undivided heart,
    that I may fear your name.

Wisdom

PSALM 111:10
The fear of the LORD is the beginning of wisdom;
all who follow his precepts have
good understanding.
To him belongs eternal praise.

ECCLESIASTES 7:11 — 12
Wisdom, like an inheritance, is a good thing
and benefits those who see the sun.
Wisdom is a shelter
as money is a shelter,
but the advantage of knowledge is this:
that wisdom preserves the life of
its possessor.

PROVERBS 24:14
Know also that wisdom is sweet to your soul;
if you find it, there is a future hope for you,
and your hope will not be cut off.

ECCLESIASTES 7:19
Wisdom makes one wise man more powerful
than ten rulers in a city.

JAMES 1:5

If any of you lacks wisdom, he should ask God,
who gives generously to all without finding fault,
and it will be given to him.

I CORINTHIANS 1:25

The foolishness of God is wiser than man's
wisdom, and the weakness of God is stronger than
man's strength.

PROVERBS 4:7

Wisdom is supreme; therefore get wisdom.
    Though it cost all you have, get understanding.

JAMES 3:17

The wisdom that comes from heaven is first of all
pure; then peace-loving, considerate, submissive,
full of mercy and good fruit, impartial and sincere.

PROVERBS 16:16

How much better to get wisdom than gold,
    to choose understanding rather than silver!

ECCLESIASTES 8:1

Who is like the wise man?
    Who knows the explanation of things?
Wisdom brightens a man's face
    and changes its hard appearance.

WORSHIP

EXODUS 15:1 — 2

Moses and the Israelites sang this song
to the LORD:
"I will sing to the LORD,
    for he is highly exalted.
The horse and its rider
    he has hurled into the sea.
The LORD is my strength and my song;
    he has become my salvation.
He is my God, and I will praise him,
    my father's God, and I will exalt him."

1 CHRONICLES 16:25

Great is the LORD and most worthy of praise;
    he is to be feared above all gods.

PSALM 29:2

Ascribe to the LORD the glory due his name;
    worship the LORD in the splendor of
    his holiness.

PSALM 95:6

Come, let us bow down in worship,
    let us kneel before the LORD our Maker.

ROMANS 12:1

I urge you, in view of God's mercy, to offer your
bodies as living sacrifices, holy and pleasing to
God—this is your spiritual act of worship.

MALACHI 4:2

"For you who revere my name," declares the LORD,
"the sun of righteousness will rise with healing in
its wings. And you will go out and leap like calves
released from the stall."

PSALM 43:4

Then will I go to the altar of God,
    to God, my joy and my delight.
I will praise you with the harp,
    O God, my God.

PSALM 100:2

Worship the LORD with gladness;
come before him with joyful songs.

HEBREWS 12:28

Since we are receiving a kingdom that cannot be
shaken, let us be thankful, and so worship God
acceptably with reverence and awe.

At Inspirio, we love to hear from you—
your stories, your feedback,
and your product ideas.
Please send your comments to us
by way of e-mail at
icares@zondervan.com
or to the address below:

Attn: Inspirio Cares
5300 Patterson Avenue SE
Grand Rapids, MI 49530

If you would like further information
about Inspirio and the products we
create, please visit us at:
www.inspiriogifts.com

Thank you and God bless!